JUST DO IT,
CRAZY OR NOT

Best Wishes
From Irvin W Hornkohl

Mary Penner

JUST DO IT, CRAZY OR NOT

**one man's
bold life
of
taking
chances
and
surviving
it all**

Mary Penner *and* Irvin Hornkohl

Manzano Alley Press

Printed and bound in the United States of America.

Library of Congress Control Number: 2011917678

ISBN 978-0-9846576-5-0

Cover photograph
by Debbie Wiens of Legacy Classics Photography

Thanks to Ruth Friesen and Tim Penner for layout assistance.

Manzano Alley Press
P.O. Box 1314
Tijeras, NM 87059
www.manzanoalley.com

If you would not be forgotten as soon as you're dead and rotten, either write things worth reading, or do things worth the writing.

Benjamin Franklin

I've been told that there were so many interesting things that happened in my life, that I shouldn't keep it to myself. Get it out. Let it all hang out.

Irvin Hornkohl

For my father who stood steadfast in the care and
unwavering love for his children.

To all the veterans who bravely served to protect and
save our country during all those trying years.
I honor them all.

I.H.

To Tim, Rachel, and Mom, my faithful supporters.
And, to Dad, whose stories live in my heart.

M.P.

Contents

"It was a dream of mine when I was a kid to get my butt out of Denver and see the world."

"The bullets were tearing up the grass fifty feet from us."

"We were happy as hell to sink a Japanese ship. They got us at Pearl and it was their turn."

"It was always an adventure. We didn't make a million, but we had fun."

"If someone squealed on me, I knew I was dead."

"We figured we were safe unless a rocket hit us."

Contents

December 7, 2006

He was the last person to board the airplane. Wearing a black cap with the name of a Navy ship stitched across the front, I could tell he was an old veteran. He nodded at the four young men in Army fatigues sitting across the aisle from me and said, "Hello, boys." Glancing at his ticket, he looked at the empty seat next to me. "I guess this is my seat." He stowed his suitcase and sat down.

I don't normally talk much to strangers on airplanes, especially at six o'clock in the morning. But, on this cold morning in December, I asked the old man, "Where are you headed today?"

"Honolulu."

"That's wonderful. Have you been there before?"

"Many times. I'm going to Pearl Harbor today. Today's the anniversary of the attack. I was there when the war started."

"You were at Pearl Harbor?"

"I sure was."

That's how I met Irvin Hornkohl, on a 6:00 a.m. flight from Albuquerque to Dallas on December 7, 2006. During the next hour and a half, Irvin talked and I listened. When the plane pulled up to the jetway in Dallas, for the first time in my life, I was sorry that my flight was over. I wanted to hear more stories.

He told me a story about being in the Civilian Conservation Corps as a teenager. My dad had also been in the CCCs and I had recently ordered his personnel file from the government. Irvin wanted to know how to get his own file, so he gave me his home address in Trinidad, Colorado. I promised to send him the information on how to order his records. That promise ensured that our chance acquaintance didn't end in the Dallas airport.

Over the next two years, we exchanged letters and my husband, daughter, and I stopped to visit Irvin and his wife a couple times when we passed through Trinidad. On a sunny September afternoon in 2008, I stood outside Irvin's ranch house, watching him toss hay to the cows. He turned to me and said, "Do you think you could write a book about my life?"

I didn't know what to say. I loved hearing his stories, but he had never mentioned the idea of writing them down.

"I've done a lot of things in my life. I think it would be interesting reading. Is that something that you could do?"

I stammered for an answer, "Well...." How could I write Irvin's life story when I hadn't written my own father's story? My dad had been a World War II Navy veteran, as well. How could I find the time to write a book? I had my own business, my own projects, and my family. How could I logistically write a book about him when we lived 250 miles apart? How could I write a biography? I'd never written one before. It was a crazy idea. How could I say no?

"Sure. I think I can do that."

M.P.

Author's Note

For the past three years, I've listened as Irvin told me the stories of his life. Using a digital recorder, I captured more than fifty hours of his stories. I then transcribed the oral stories, often pulling bits and pieces of the same story from several different recordings. After transcribing each story, I gave them shape and cohesion, editing and adding details for clarity. We have read and discussed each story numerous times. Irvin is a natural storyteller. The stories in this book mimic the texture and tone of his storytelling voice.

Irvin is eighty-eight years old. These stories are his memories of events that occurred as long as eighty years ago. Undoubtedly, some of the details may not be completely accurate. We have tried to verify events and names of places and people as much as possible. However, this is not intended to be a history book based on documented evidence. This is a book of Irvin's memories of history as he experienced it. Whatever he says about people, places, and events, constitute his opinions and his recollections of how the events transpired.

M.P.

December 7, 1941

I bailed out of bed pretty early. It was almost like any other day except it was a Sunday. I didn't have to go to work or to school. So I leisurely took a shower and got ready to go down to breakfast. I headed down the stairs and into the mess hall. Other guys were up. There were quite a few in the mess hall. After I got done eating about a quarter of eight, I started outside. I stood there looking around; it was a beautiful morning. No clouds, just a beautiful day to be in Hawaii.

Then all of a sudden I heard this machine gun fire going off. This plane came right over the barracks and let off quite a row of bullets. We just stood there in amazement at first. We couldn't believe this was happening. I looked up and saw those big red meatballs on the wings.

"Hell, that's Japs!"

PART I
YOUNG DREAMS
1923 – 1941

*"It was a dream of mine when I
was a kid to get my butt out of
Denver and see the world."*

Touch One of Them Kids and I'll Kill You

I was born at home on December 8, 1923 in Denver, Colorado. Actually the area of Denver where I grew up was called Barnum, because P.T. Barnum, the circus man, had his winter quarters there. We used to call ourselves the Barnum mud-slingers because of the roads. We just had dirt roads at that time. When the roads got wet, that mud would be up over the tops of your shoes.

My dad grew up in Nebraska. His name was Albert August Hornkohl. He had a third grade education; he was almost illiterate. He had to work his fanny off. He held all kinds of jobs. He was a wonderful teamster. He knew horses inside out. He could do anything with a horse. He even worked for a circus one time as a horse trainer. He worked for the railroad. And, he farmed. That's the way it was with Dad. He did all kinds of work.

When he was a young man in Nebraska, he got in a fight and popped a guy on the head. He didn't kill him or anything, but Dad had to leave town. His railroad friends got him out of town on a caboose and that's how he ended up in Colorado.

His brother, my Uncle Bill, had a farm in southern Colorado and he ran a big thrashing machine from Kansas into Nebraska, thrashing wheat. My dad went to work with his brother. They were thrashing wheat in Kansas, and one day, Dad met my mom, Eva May Hughes, and they were attracted to one another. Now, he wasn't a kid; well, he wasn't old, either. He was probably thirty-eight or thirty-nine. Never been married.

My mom already had a daughter named Faye. Mom wasn't married before, though, not to my knowledge. She came back to Colorado with my dad. They had three kids together, and I was the last; there was my brother Everett and my sister Emma before me. I was an illegitimate child; we all were. My parents weren't married. They lived together for about eight years before they finally split up and went different directions.

I was about a year old when my parents had a big ruckus, a big fight in the kitchen. There were pots and pans flying all over; so they split up. Faye went with Mom and we three stayed with Dad.

Mom and her boyfriend came back to our house to get us and take us with her. There was another ruckus. My dad said, "You touch one of them kids and I'll kill you. You get out of this house right now. These kids are staying here."

They came another time or two, but Dad would meet them with his *pistola*. After awhile, she quit trying to get us kids.

Dad had an awful time. He had housekeepers and babysitters, one after another. Neighbors would help take care of us, too. One time, somebody sent the special services, child welfare, whatever it was called in those days. They tried to take us away. There was another ruckus, and out came the pistol. Eventually, they all left us alone.

From audio recordings made on March 26, 2009 and January 19, 2010.

Albert Hornkohl with children, l-r: Everett, Emma, Irvin

Our Tarpaper Shack

Dad had two lots of land in Denver at 225 South Julian. We lived in a house that my dad built. He put it all together from railroad boxcars. The railroad would sell these old boxcars. He'd pay five or ten dollars and he got the boxcar. Dad dismantled these boxcars to get lumber to build our house.

People who lived in Barnum used to say, "Your dad? I remember he used to go up the street here with big loads of lumber on his shoulder."

He'd bring that lumber home from work on the streetcar and bit by bit he built our house. It had four rooms, one story with a flat roof. It was real solid, but Dad used to call it our tarpaper shack. We had a big pot-bellied stove in the living room. It was a real warm house. There were two bedrooms and a kitchen. My sister and my brother both had beds in one little bedroom. Dad dug a basement down below. It was a dirt basement. Well, it wasn't really a basement; it was just a hole in the ground underneath the house. It was probably about eight feet by eight feet, with a door on it. They put a bed down there for me. It was fixed up nice; it was clean even though the walls and the floor were dirt. Once I went to bed, they didn't see me until the next morning. It was awful easy for me to slip away at night.

From audio recordings made on March 26, 2009 and January 19, 2010.

She Played Her Cards Wrong

I never really knew my mom's side of the family. My dad would hardly allow us to see them. There was so much hatred in his heart for my mom. He never really talked about it, but I knew it was there. My mom broke his heart. That was about the worst thing that ever happened to him – my mother. I knew that if I ever left Dad to be with her that would break him up even more. So, because I loved my dad, I just didn't press the issue about my mom.

I never saw her when I was a kid. I had no idea what she looked like. She didn't come around. She was probably afraid of my dad. One Christmas she sent us some presents. Some old and dirty dolls and toys. Well-worn. I expect it was all she could afford. She was probably trying to make some amends. She wrote to me a couple of times during the war, but I didn't write back to her.

I saw her a few times after I came out of the Navy. After I got married, my mother-in-law knew my mother somehow. They were friends.

One night my mother-in-law said to me, "Irvin, we've been invited to your mother's house for dinner. Now, we're going, aren't we?"

"Well, I guess we are."

We went to my mom's house for dinner. It was a nice spread. We just visited over dinner and that was about it.

My mother never had good luck with men. She was with one fellow for quite awhile. Then she moved on and had another husband. And she had three more kids. I met my half-sister and my two half-brothers a couple of times. I think my half-sister is dead now. I don't know about the two brothers.

This first fellow, the guy she left my dad for, was rotten. He raped my half-sister Faye and left her for dead out in a cornfield. She somehow lived through it. That SOB went to prison; they put his butt in the cooler. Faye was taken away from my mother and put in a foster home. She stayed there

5

until she was eighteen. Then they told her she had to get out on her own. She had nowhere to go. She wouldn't go back to my mother's place, so she contacted my dad. Dad went to get her. He felt an obligation to her. He'd been a step-dad to her years before. That's the way he was, if somebody needed help, he would do what he could.

We drove out to Nebraska to get her. She was staying on the most beautiful farm I'd ever seen. They had great big silos and a big barn. They had beautiful horses. I wanted to stay.

"Dad, I'd like to stay here." I was probably about nine or ten years old at the time.

"No, you're going home with me, son."

We all went home together and Faye stayed with us until she was able to go out on her own.

Later on, after I was an adult, I got to know my mother's sister. Apparently, she used to babysit me before my mom left home.

"Your mom was quite a rounder," my aunt told me. "It always fell on me to babysit you when she went out to make the rounds of the bars."

I don't think my mother was a bad woman. I just think she played her cards wrong a few times. I never really made any effort to get close to her. I'm kind of sorry I didn't. You can't go back and put those things right.

From audio recordings made on October 10, 2009 and February 17, 2011.

We Almost Dropped in the Dirt

Mrs. Jordan was the only mother I ever knew. She came to live with us when I was about five or six years old. She was a tall woman from the Ozarks in Missouri. She was a widow with a daughter and a son. My dad and Mrs. Jordan never married. But, she was like our step-mother, without all the formalities. She was a wonderful mother. She was always good to us. My sister called her Mother Jordan. I called her Mom. She was Mom.

She used to tell me stories about the riverboats on the Mississippi River. How these gamblers would be thrown over the side for cheating at cards. Those were scary stories for a little kid. She'd say, "You know, Irvin, those gamblers would crawl up the riverbanks, and they'd get almost to the top and then they'd slide back down into the water."

She took us up to Idaho two or three summers and we stayed with her daughter and son-in-law. Dad stayed in Colorado, working his job on the railroad and running that little farm we had. My brother worked in the Idaho potato fields. I helped out, too. I had a little deal going where I would go and round up a sack full of sawdust and take it to town and sell it to the butchers. The butchers put sawdust on the floors. I'd get fifty cents a sack. I was just ten or eleven years old.

Ma Jordan had a son named Douglas. He was my buddy. He was big and good-looking. He was about ten years older than me. He was a professional boxer, a real good one. He taught me how to fight. Some of the kids at school were picking on me. You know how kids are. He said, "Here's the way you do it, Irvin." He showed me a move or two.

I was never a good fighter like Douglas, but I did the best I could. I would fight until I dropped on the ground if I had to. There were some kids in the neighborhood named Ludlow. My brother had trouble with the older Ludlow kid, and I had trouble with the younger Ludlow kid. One day when I was about twelve, I was in the public library there

7

in Barnum. There wasn't any air conditioning and it was a hot day, so I was hanging out by the window reading a book. This Ludlow kid came walking by the window and he said something to me. And I said something back. Just dumb kid talk, trying to sound tough.

"You want to take me on?" he said.

"Not really. What do you think?"

"I don't think you can whip me," he said.

"I think I can."

"Well, let's go over to the big empty lot and find out."

There was a big lot at the corner of Knox and First Avenue. We got over there and we squared off and started throwing punches at each other. We fought until we almost dropped in the dirt. I was just praying for somebody to come along and stop this fight. I wanted somebody to get me out of this predicament. I was getting as many licks on him as he was on me. We were pretty well matched, but, still, I'd had enough. There was a ring of kids around us, cheering us on. But, nobody tried to stop us.

"Ludlow," I said. "Let's give it up."

Neither one of us wanted to quit. But, we finally walked off and went to our homes. We were both bloody and bruised. The minute I walked into the house, Ma Jordan said, "What'd the other guy look like?" She was used to seeing Douglas come home pretty well bunged up after a fight.

Douglas left town when I was still pretty young. He came up to me one day and said, "Irvin, I'm leaving town."

"No, Douglas, you can't go."

"I've got to go. There's nothing for me here in Denver."

"I'll sure miss you." I think I was crying a little.

"I'll come back and see you." He patted me on the head and left. I hardly ever saw him again. He married a lady in Nevada whose family was in politics. I heard that he once ran for governor of Nevada.

From audio recordings made on March 25, 2009, March 26, 2009, and June 12, 2011.

We're Taking on Water

Growing up in Denver, I always wanted to see what was on the other side of the mountains. I wanted to see the world. I really did. It was a dream of mine when I was a kid to get my butt out of Denver and see the world. I was always a soft touch for things like running away or going over the mountain. I loved my dad; there was no reason to leave home. He didn't beat up on me. I just wanted adventure.

Me and the three Beeson kids who lived in my neighborhood built a raft one time. We made it out of scrap lumber. It had wheels on it, too, from a baby carriage. We were going to pull this raft up over the mountains and launch it in the Pacific Ocean. These were kid dreams. Big dreams. We thought we were big-time Charlies. We asked some people around the neighborhood if this raft was seaworthy. Everybody said, "That will never float."

We never even got this raft on the road. But the dream was in my brain that I was going to make it over that mountain and find the Pacific Ocean. So, I tried to build a canoe the next time.

Me and Jack McFee, the kid from across the street, made this canoe out of an eight foot sheet of tin roofing. We folded it up to be like a canoe. We put wood in the front, and we put more wood in the back to close up the ends. That sheeting had a whole bunch of holes in it. So, we plugged tar into the holes and tried to make it waterproof.

Then we went to the frog pond to launch the canoe. It wasn't a very big pond, but we used to go swimming in it and it was deep. There were a bunch of people there that day, swimming and fishing. Everybody watched us lug our canoe down to the water.

"Irvin," they said, "that ain't gonna float."

"Oh yeah. It'll float."

We climbed in and shoved off. We were busily chew tar that we'd gathered from the road, getting it ni gushy to plug up the holes if we sprung any leaks. Well, it leaked all right. We got about half way across the frog pond, and I said, "Jack, we're taking on water!"

Water was coming in everywhere. We slapped that tar onto the holes, but we were stupid. We tried plugging the holes on the inside of the canoe instead of the outside. Outside, there would have been pressure up against the side and that might have held the tar onto the hole. Inside, those bits of tar popped off and the water shot right through the holes.

"We'll be all right, Irvin," Jack said. "Paddle!"

Of course, we didn't have any oars; we had to paddle with our hands. We were really getting with it, too. At that time I didn't know how to swim very well. That was a problem. The canoe went down. Glug, glug – sunk, right in the middle of the fish pond. Luckily, Felix Dominic, an older kid from the neighborhood, was sitting on the bank and he saw me sinking. Felix dove in and grabbed me by the neck and dragged me to shore.

"Irvin, you crazy kid." I couldn't disagree with him.

From audio recordings made on March 26, 2009 and June 16, 2009.

He Was Badder than Bad

The Santa Fe Railroad tracks weren't very far from Barnum. A lot of people were on the move during the Depression. Some of them camped out in the hobo jungles near the tracks. We'd go down there and talk to them.

"Where you going?"

"We're going to California." They all wanted to go to California. They caught these freights out of town, ending up who knows where.

Jack McFee lived across the street from us with his mother. He was two or three years older than me. He and I got along okay. I guess he was a bad influence on me. I mean he was badder than bad. To say he was a thief would be putting it mildly. Jack knew from his brother Joe how to catch these freights. Joe went to California two or three times riding freight trains and he told Jack all about it. Jack was an eager listener. One day Jack talked me into going down to the hobo jungle with him.

"Irvin," he said, "we're gonna get on a freight train and go to California."

"We are?"

I couldn't have been much older than ten. So, we went down there that night; it was darker than sin. We sized up the freight train that was going to take us to California. We hid in the jungle waiting. We could see them working on the train, getting it all bunched up in the yard. They were getting ready to pull out and I remember seeing the lights in the caboose. Jack's brother had told him if you see the lights on in the caboose that means the train is about ready to leave. So, we started getting all anxious and ready to go. There were a few hobos getting ready to mount up, too.

The train started pulling out. We ran out there, and I mean my little short legs were just churning. I had to use all my muscles to leap up and get on that first rung of the ladder. We climbed the ladder up to the top of the boxcar. And, you know, what a couple of dumbbells we were. We

11

only had one jacket with us and that was mine. It was late in the fall, and it was cold on top of the boxcar. So, we had to swap off my jacket to keep from freezing on that darn boxcar. Jack said, "Oh, I'm cold. Let me have the jacket for awhile." Jack didn't have a jacket. Half the time he didn't have shoes. Even in the winter.

All night the train made stops. They couldn't go very far because they had to stop and get water and coal. We made four or five stops. Finally, we pulled into Pueblo the next morning. They were getting ready to break up the train and kick out the cars that were destined for Pueblo. We jumped down. Hungry, man, we were hungry. The sun was out. It felt great and it started to warm us up. That's when the long arm of the law reached out and grabbed us. Railroad security guards picked us up right in the rail yard and took us to the station house.

"What are you kids doing?" they asked.

"Well, we're going to California."

"No you're not. You're going home."

First, they were going to call our parents. But, for some reason, they didn't. They said, "You kids know how to get back home?"

"Yeah. Get on the highway, I guess."

We were used to hitchhiking. That's the way everybody got around in those days. So, they let us go. We started hitchhiking and got a couple of rides. We got put out somewhere, who knows where it was, and we were hungry. We went up to this house and knocked on the door. A lady came to the door and we asked her if we could have some milk because she had three or four bottles of milk sitting on her porch. She gave us a bottle of milk and some bread. We were sure grateful for that. We got another ride and ended up in Castle Rock. Castle Rock was just a little town back then. There was a filling station and little diner there. We went in the diner. Of course, we were filthy and had coal dust all over us.

The guy behind the counter said, "How long since you kids ate?"

"Days ago." We were hungry. "We ain't got no money."

"I know that. Just looking at you I can tell you ain't got no money."

He came out with ham and eggs and potatoes and fed us. We devoured that real fast. He got us a ride with a trucker going into Denver. We rode with him to Denver and he let us out not too far from home. We walked on home. We'd been gone three days. My dad had no idea where we were. He knew that Jack from across the street was gone, too, so he figured we'd gone off together. My dad hated Jack with a passion. When we came straggling home Dad was so glad to see me, he didn't even whip me.

We hopped freights a couple more times. We didn't get very far out of town. We got to Greeley one time before we got tossed off. We'd get back out on the highway and ask which way was Denver, then we'd just put our thumbs out and hitchhike back home.

The last time I tried to hop a train with Jack didn't work out. On boxcars, there were two sets of ladders. One ladder went to the top of the boxcar, and there was another ladder on the back end that had only two steps. We dashed out to hop this freight and I grabbed the ladder on the back end with the two steps and Jack got on the ladder with the steps to the top. So he went on up the ladder onto the top, and I was stuck on the ladder with just two steps. All the time the train was picking up speed; it was going like the dickens. I thought, well, I'll jump off and grab the next boxcar. I jumped off and slammed right into a switch stand. That knocked the crap out of me. I rolled over and saw Jack up on top riding off. I went back home. Jack came home three or four days later.

"What happened to you?" he asked.

I told him what happened. I didn't care for hopping trains anymore.

From audio recordings made on March 26, 2009, January 10, 2010, and January 19, 2010.

13

Picking Nails Out of Our Feet

We moved back and forth a few times between the house in Barnum and a farm. We rented several different farms. We went to these farms to grow big gardens. Dad was trying to put food on the table and feed us kids. You could hardly have much of a garden in town. Dad wasn't really a city man, anyway. He always wanted to be on a farm, with animals, and growing crops. One farm we rented was in Adams City. There was an old house on the farm and before we moved there someone had replaced the roof. They'd taken that old shingle roof off and the whole yard around the house was full of nails. We were constantly picking nails out of our feet, which wasn't very pretty. We never wore shoes in the summer. We didn't have money for shoes.

The last farm we rented was up near Broomfield, up north of Denver. There was nothing in Broomfield in those days, except a granary, a filling station, a post office, and a beer joint. Our farm was actually in a place called Semper. Semper was just a railroad stop, really.

My dad rented out the house in Barnum for twenty-five dollars a month and that money paid the rent for the farm in Broomfield. We had about forty acres. There was an old, two-story house on the place. We put in more than an acre of garden. Ma Jordan canned everything we grew in that garden. We had a little apple orchard, too. We had chickens and a couple of beef cattle. We'd get a few calves, and I had to feed them and take care of them and watch them grow. Then all of a sudden, one of the cows wouldn't be there. It went to the slaughter house. We raised five or six pigs in the hog pen all the time. We'd butcher them, too. Dad did the butchering and Mrs. Jordan would smoke the meat.

I started the first grade in Broomfield in mid-year, for some reason. I'm not sure why I didn't start at the beginning of the year. Those kids out there were a mean bunch. The new kid was new pickin's. I got picked on an awful lot. My brother had to defend me. He was five years older and

14

he could take ahold of those mean kids and shake them off me.

Then we moved back to Barnum where I went to Barnum School. It was a big brick building, a nice school. There were eight grades. I remember many of my teachers; they were all lady teachers except one man.

My buddy Jack hated school with a passion. He always tried to get me to play hookey. I did once. All we did was hide all day.

I said, "I ain't doing this anymore, Jack. If I've got to go sit in the culvert and hide all day, I'd rather go to school."

Plus, you had to worry about making up a fake note from your parents to take to the teacher. Why, she could just look at those notes and know they were fake.

Jack got into trouble at school all the time. Mostly petty stuff. Our principal was Mr. Richel. He was a heavy set, stocky man, with horn-rimmed glasses. I'd been sent to his office a couple of times for doing something or other, and I always thought he was a nice guy, fair and not too mean.

One day Jack showed me a gun.

He said, "I'm gonna kill Mr. Richel."

"You are not. Why would you want to do that?"

Jack complained that Mr. Richel did this and did that to him. Jack was ornery, yet he blamed Mr. Richel whenever he got punished. I should have run right on down to the school and told them Jack had a gun. But, in those times, you didn't squeal on anybody.

Jack took this gun and he went down there to shoot Mr. Richel. I didn't really believe that Jack was going to do it, or I would have broken the rules and squealed on him. Mr. Richel got the gun away from him somehow. I don't think Jack ever went back to school again. I pretty much washed out on Jack after that. Didn't hang out with him anymore.

Eventually we moved out to the farm in Broomfield for good. We lost the house in Barnum. I'm not exactly sure of all the details. I can remember my dad and Mrs. Jordan sitting at the kitchen table paying bills and they came to the bill for the property. My dad was forever in debt trying to pay off the land where he built our house. Ma Jordan kept saying, "Don't pay it, Red." That was Dad's nickname, Red. There were so many bills and so little money. I think Ma Jordan was instrumental in us losing the house. My sister always said the house was stolen from us.

Whatever it was with the house, we left Denver and went out to the farm. I finished school in the one room schoolhouse in Broomfield. I went through the eighth grade.

Dad said, "You better go to high school."

"Well, Dad," I said, "how am I going to get to Arvada?" That was where the high school was and it was six miles away. Dad had to take the car to work in Denver and it wasn't in the same direction as the high school. In those days, a lot of people didn't go past the eighth grade. So, that was the extent of my education.

From audio recordings made on March 26, 2009, June 17, 2009, and January 19, 2010.

Mad as a Dickens about These Chickens

This is a part of my life that I don't like to talk about. Mrs. Jordan could be an ornery old gal when she wanted to be. When I was about fifteen or sixteen years old, we were living on the farm and Mrs. Jordan told me to go outside and work on the chickens, clean out the coops, put out fresh feed, that sort of thing. Well, I either ignored her or thought I was too busy doing something else.

She said, "Have you taken care of those chickens?"

I gave a smart remark about the chickens and made a few excuses about why I didn't want to tend the chickens. So we got into an argument, and, by the minute, she was getting madder and madder at me. Then she grabbed a stove lifter. A stove lifter is a cast iron rod that you insert into a hole in the stove lid to lift it off. She started beating me on the head with the stove lifter. I took quite a beating. Actually, she beat the hell out of me. Her daughter, Helen, was there and had ahold of me. I didn't do anything to defend myself. I covered my head as best as I could. I never raised a hand to her. She was just mad as a dickens about these chickens. Finally, I got out of the house and went to the neighbors. I was bleeding pretty bad. They dumped a bucket of water on my head and then took me to the doctor in Golden. They put twenty-one stitches in my head.

Then they sent me to a foster home. A real nice lady was there along with her husband. She showed me to a room and said, "This is your room." I thought, man, this ain't so bad. It was the first time in my life I slept on a bed with sheets. I didn't know what a sheet was. We always just slept with a quilt on the mattress. I was there a week and then she said, "Irvin, you have to go to court this morning." She ironed my pants and I was as clean as could be. They had a bathtub and all this wonderful stuff in their house.

So, I went to court. They didn't put my parents on trial. They were just trying to get to the bottom of it. Dad was awfully worried. I could tell by looking at him sitting there.

Mrs. Jordon didn't seem too sorry about what she did. In her mind, she was supposedly right.

The judge asked me, "Do you want to go home?"

"Yes. I want to go home."

"With your mother and father?"

"Yes, with my mother and father."

"Do you really want to go? You tell me right now."

"I want it worse than anything in this world."

That was the only time something like that ever happened. I don't know what set her off. I think she was already mad about something and just took it out on me. She and my father had strained relations after that, though. One day she said, "I've got a job in town working in a cannery." She rode back and forth for awhile. Then finally she moved out and got an apartment.

Then she said to me, "There's this sheet metal company that's looking for an apprentice. Would you like to go to work for them?" I'd never done that sort of thing, but I figured I'd try it. She said I could live with her and her daughter and granddaughter. I went and lived with them and worked at the sheet metal company. I made twelve dollars a week and I gave Mrs. Jordan eight dollars.

We got along great. I think we both just let everything go under the bridge. We never held a grudge. I lived with Mrs. Jordan about a year. She got annoyed with me because in the evenings I would go and hang out at the pool hall. She didn't think I should be doing that. But, she knew she didn't really have too much say in what I did. She could have kicked me out of her apartment if she wanted to, I suppose. Eventually I was laid off from the sheet metal company and went back to the farm with my dad. Life then wasn't easy. The life I had wasn't easy. I had a loving father, but the rest of life's circumstances hardened me for the rougher times that were coming.

From audio recordings made on March 25, 2009, March 26, 2009, and October 10, 2009.

Nobody Was Crying about the Hard Labor

Just after my seventeenth birthday, I went into the Civilian Conservation Corps in January of 1941. We called it the CCs or the CC camps. It was still the time of the Depression, really. The wind had blown half of this country away during the 1930s. And we were poor, just like about everybody else. President Roosevelt put together this CC camp program to put young men to work. Get them off the streets and help them earn some money.

So, I joined and I was assigned to a camp in Idaho Springs, Colorado — up in the mountains, up in the real Rockies. They took us up there in a Dodge truck and dumped us out. We lived in barracks made out of plywood with tarpaper stuck to the outside. There was a pot-bellied stove in the center of the room. There were about forty guys in the barracks. It was brutally cold at times, but that didn't stop us from going to work every day. They gave us old Army uniforms to wear. Wool pants, shirts, and overcoats.

When I went in the CCs, I'd been raised partially on the farm and partially in the city. Growing up in west Denver was no picnic. There were fights on the streets at times, lots of rough people around. I thought you had to have a tough attitude to live, considering the environment I came from. When I was thrown into the CCs, it was a different life. It was a lot like the military. They expected discipline and you had to show respect to your supervisors. They really stressed hygiene. Cleanliness. We didn't have a lot of hygiene in my house when I was growing up. We weren't totally uncouth, but we never took showers. We hardly ever took a bath, maybe once a week and that was in a big tub on the kitchen floor.

I had a couple of bad moments in the CCs, mainly at the first. I had this attitude and I wasn't used to taking orders. I had a little flair up with the barracks supervisor one time.

We'd been out all day, working hard, and he said to me, "Get in there and take a shower."

I gave him a bit of a smart remark. "I'll take a shower when I'm damn well ready."

That didn't go over well. He fined me a dollar. In those days, a buck was pretty serious money. That was my whole pay for the day's work. We made a dollar a day and at the end of the month, they sent twenty-two dollars of our pay back to our parents. So, we only got to keep eight dollars a month. Losing that dollar over not wanting to take a shower was an eye opener. I'm rough at the edges, rougher than a cob. But, I'm not stupid. I could see that I needed to play along, follow the rules, and things would get better for me.

We did all kinds of work in the forest. We planted trees. I learned how to chop logs and skin the bark off of them. We built latrines out of logs. I just about cut off my foot one time, skinning those logs with a sharp adz. I swung that big blade down there and I missed the log and slammed it on the top of my foot. I was wearing boots, of course. I kept on working and before long, my foot started to feel soggy inside my boot. I thought, this isn't good. I went to the medic. We pulled off my boot and the blood came pouring out. There was a pretty good cut along the top of my foot. But I didn't crack the bones or anything. He stitched up my foot. The next day I was out working again. If that blow had landed just slightly to the side and done more serious damage, I might have been crippled for the rest of my life.

We spent a lot of time working on improving the roads up into the mountains. We used picks and shovels and jackhammers. We didn't have any big road graders. It was all hand work. Hauling dirt and rocks with a wheelbarrow. Nobody was crying about the hard labor. Nobody said, "Oh, you're taking advantage of us." We knew we had a good thing going. If it hadn't been for the CCs a lot of us would have been in trouble. No money, no jobs, no food.

Every morning one of us had to take a turn at getting up before five o'clock and tromp over to the mess hall. We had to light up the big wood burning stoves and get them good and hot before the cook came in there to fix breakfast. Well, one morning I overslept. I was supposed to have those fires going by five o'clock. I woke up about an hour late and dashed over there to the kitchen. Fortunately, the cook hadn't come in yet. I threw that wood in the stoves and I poured a whole bunch of extra fire starting fuel onto the wood. I backed off and threw a match on there. It lit up with a big whoosh and blew the lids off the stove. Those fires were burning fast and hard. I was afraid the kitchen was going to catch on fire. There was a fire extinguisher there. I grabbed it and put the fire out and then restarted it the normal way without all the extra starter fuel. I got it going just in the nick of time. The cook came in there and said, "You're a little late getting that fire built."

"I'm sorry." Better late than burning down the whole camp.

We spent a long time working on this remote road and we came to this old prospector's house. He lived in a cabin. He was a real recluse. He hadn't bathed in a long, long time. Most recluses don't like anybody coming around. But, he had an old car and this car was sitting on the road where we needed to work. We knocked on his door and told him we had to move his car.

"Move my car?"

"Yeah, we've got to push this road up through here in case somebody wants to come up and see you."

"I don't want to see anybody."

But, he agreed that we could push his car out of the way because it wouldn't start. He came outside. There were four or five of us and we started pushing this car off the road. It was a big old thing, heavy as a truck. While we were moving the car, the old man slipped and fell down and bruised his knee. We picked him up and dusted him off. He was hurt. He was crying and the tears coming down his cheeks were cutting furrows through the dirt on his face. We took care of him the best we could.

As time went on, we got the road past his place. We'd see him every day and we'd talk to him when we could. He was such a personable and nice man. He was salt of the earth. He'd been up there mining for years. I don't know if he ever made any money at it. One day he looked kind of sickly. We asked him about it.

"Oh, I get these days once in awhile where I don't feel too good."

The next day we didn't see him, so we got worried. We went in his little cabin and we found him, dead. Somehow, we got ahold of his son who was a lawyer. He came up there on the new road that we built in his great big Cadillac.

"We were friends with your dad," we told him.

"Friends with him?"

"Yes, we thought a lot of that old guy."

He couldn't believe that anybody could like his dad. I thought, what a ding dong this guy is. He looked around his dad's old cabin and said, "Take anything in here you want."

"We don't want your dad's stuff."

The son didn't even think enough of his father to go in there and clean out his cabin. We all thought it was pretty sad. He sent someone up to take the old prospector's body away.

I had good moments in the CCs. I made some good friends. I got three meals a day. It sure wasn't bad. All of us guys in the CCs didn't know it at the time, but that experience was preparing us to grow up and take on a war. I got out of the CCs in June of 1941.

From audio recordings made on March 26, 2009, June 16, 2009, and June 12, 2011.

Now Sign Here

When I left the CCs, I never dreamed that six months later, I'd be at Pearl Harbor. I'd started to sign up for another six months in the CCs, but I thought, no, maybe I'll join the Navy. But, right when I got out of the CCs, some other guys from the camp said, "We're going to work on the railroad. Why don't you go with us?"

"Doing what?"

"They're laying track over in Price, Utah."

"You're kidding."

"No. They got work trains and sleeping cars and everything. We're going to work on section gangs."

"I don't know. That's a tough job. I'll talk to my dad."

So I asked Dad, "What do you think, Pop?"

"Well, I've done everything on the railroad," he said. "I've worked on section gangs. I'm going to let you decide. There's no work around here."

So, the next day I told my buddies I'd sign up, too. I went down to the railroad office and fibbed about my age. I told them I was eighteen. I don't know if they really even cared if I was eighteen or not. I got the job. There were four of us. Bill Bowman, Bill Foster, Frank Cox, and me.

We took out one night on the train toward Pueblo. We sat in a coach that had prisoners on it. They were on their way to the prison at Canon City. In those days the prison at Canon City was pretty notorious. They busted rocks and did other hard labor. They didn't sit around watching television like they do now. I think the prison there now is like a lounge. Pretty easy living.

Anyway, these prisoners were trying to sell everything they had. Their shoes, belt buckles, shirts. They didn't need anything where they were going.

"Who'll give me a dollar for this hat?" There were some nice Stetson hats. I was in on some of the bidding; I bought a belt. Some of the other guys bought hats and wallets, that sort of stuff. So, we spent all our money on the train buying stuff from these prisoners.

They unloaded all the prisoners, and then the next morning we ended up in Price, Utah. Man, I'd never seen any place more desolate than that. Actually, Price was a nice little town, but it sure was remote.

We went right to work laying tracks. We worked a few days and we all got together one night. The guys were complaining about their hands. They had worked them raw. I was a wheelbarrow man in the CC camps, so my hands were hardened.

They said, "We're going home."

"We just got here," I said.

"Well, we don't like it."

"How about staying a few more days and make a little bit of money?"

"Nope. We're going home. What about you?"

"Well, you ain't gonna leave me here. How much money do you all have?"

We hadn't drawn a paycheck, yet, so we pulled out all our money and put it in a little pile. We counted about a $1.35 amongst the four of us. Can you imagine? Out of four able-bodied men, that was pretty pathetic. They had a little store in one of the boxcars. You could buy bread, cigarettes, sardines, just basic stuff. We spent all our money buying a couple loaves of bread and two or three cans of sardines.

The next day the freight train came through and stopped on the siding. We hopped the freight. We had the good luck of riding in a cattle car. This car still had some hay in it. Man, that was nice. Better than those hard wooden benches we sat on in the coach going out there. There were four hobos at the other end of the car. They looked like pretty rough customers. We thought, well, if they try to take our sardines away from us, we'll put up a good fight. Four against four. We weren't giving up our bread and sardines to those hobos. They kind of eyeballed us, but they didn't do anything.

24

We zipped on down the line and went through the Moffat Tunnel, which is about six miles long. I put everything I could find across my mouth and nose and eyes. The smoke from the train was terrible. I didn't figure it would kill me, but it was very unpleasant. We eventually ended up in Denver. We'd been gone about a week. Dad was surprised to see me.

"Well," he said, "you didn't like it, huh?"

"It was all right with me, Pop, but they were going to leave me up there."

"Chalk it up to experience."

I knew I had to figure out how to make my way in this world. I said to my dad, "I need to start something that's going to help me through life. You worked on the railroad all your life. I need to find something for my life."

I was still just seventeen, but I knew I wasn't getting anywhere. I went down to the courthouse and talked to the Navy people there about signing up. They gave me a physical and decided I was sound, healthy enough.

I said to the chief signing people up, "Will you accept me?"

"Yeah, you're breathing. We'll take you. You'll have to bring your father in."

I took Dad down there. He took the afternoon off from work. Dad said to the chief, "How much time can you give the boy?"

"We don't give them time around here. We sign them up."

"Okay."

Dad knew nothing about the Navy. He'd just been a hard worker his whole life, trying to put food on the table.

"Now sign here," he said to Dad.

Dad was practically illiterate, but he could sign his name. Whenever he had to sign something, he made a big show of it. He was real deliberate about it. He got the pen in his hand and he signed his name on my enlistment paper. It was beautiful handwriting for someone who could barely read.

I went in the Navy on July 1, 1941. I was seventeen and a half years old. I enlisted for four years. I had wanted to see the world from the time I was a little kid. I wanted adventure. For poor guys like me, the Navy was the only way to do that in those days. Joining the Navy probably saved my life. I was going nowhere in Denver.

From audio recordings made on March 26, 2009, June 16, 2009, June 17, 2009, October 9, 2009, and February 18, 2011.

PART II
THE NAVY & PEARL HARBOR
1941

*"The bullets were tearing up the
grass fifty feet from us."*

A Battleship for My First Assignment

They gave me a train ticket to San Diego, California. I left within a few days after I signed up. They were shuffling us out to San Diego as quick as they could get us on a train. By this time, it was just me and my dad living together, and he had to work that day.

He said, "You can handle it, son."

"I can take it from here, Pop."

I went down to the train station by myself. There were a few other Navy guys on the train, too. They were waving from the train at their folks, hollering goodbye. I didn't have anyone there to wave to.

Most of my train travel had been on top of a boxcar or stowing away in an empty cattle car. This train trip was in high style. I had my own sleeper. Beautiful quarters. I got meal tickets, too. I thought, man, I've hit the jackpot. In the dining car, the waiters would come around and say, "What would you like, sir?" We had some wonderful food.

The trip took about two days. I was pretty excited when we rolled through Phoenix. I'd never seen country like that. Then I finally got to see California. The train went through Los Angeles and then turned south. I got to see the ocean for the first time through the train window.

I finally arrived at the San Diego Naval Training Station. To me, boot camp was wonderful. I was ready to do whatever they told me to. Man, they put us through the paces. I wore out two pairs of shoes from all the marching. The soles were completely gone. They taught us how to tie knots and how to mend rope. We went out to the firing range. We practiced firing the 30-06 rifle, a bolt action. One shot at a time. I got good marks on the rifle range.

We couldn't leave the base during boot camp. Except, I got out one afternoon. My sister Emma was married to an Army officer and they were stationed out near Riverside, California. Emma and Maurice came down to San Diego one Sunday. Maurice was all decked out in his lieutenant's uniform. He got ahold of my company chief in his office.

"We only have a few hours," Maurice told him. "We want to take him to the zoo if you'll give us permission to take him off the base. I'll be responsible for him."

"Well, that's irregular. We don't normally allow recruits off the base."

Maurice started swinging a little rank and he finally persuaded the chief to let me go. Boy, I got my whites on and dashed out to their car and there was this pretty girl sitting in the back seat. They'd brought along a date for me, the daughter of another Army officer. I was real surprised.

We went to the zoo. I'd never been to a zoo before. It was beautiful. They had every kind of animal there. We had a wonderful time that day. I promised to write this girl. I don't think I ever did.

Boot camp lasted about four weeks. Toward the end, I ran to the bulletin board every day to see if my name was on the assignment list. One day I went up to the bulletin board and I ran my finger down that long list. I saw my name, Hornkohl, Irvin W., USS *Oklahoma*.

My God, a battleship for my first assignment. I couldn't ask for anything better than that. I thought, man, now I'm going to get out there on that ocean. Everything was turning out real well. I told myself, I'm going to make myself the best damn sailor in the Navy. This was my chance to be somebody.

From audio recordings made on February 18, 2011 and April 22, 2011.

Like a Real Sailor

I came right straight out of boot camp and took the train up to Oakland, California. About eight or ten of us from camp were assigned to the USS *Oklahoma*. We were all apprentice seamen. The *Oklahoma* was sitting in the dry docks. I never saw such a massive ship in all my life. I had a seabag; it had all my clothes and gear in it. And, in those days you hauled around a hammock made out of sturdy canvas. You had to put your seabag inside your hammock and then you lashed it together with eight half-hitches. Be like a real sailor and lash your gear down. When it was all put together, it looked sort of like a canoe.

We went on the docks and up to the gangplank that went across to the *Oklahoma*. The gangplank wasn't very wide and there were just two little strands of rope to hold on to, one on each side. I looked down and it was a big drop down to the bottom of that dry dock. I had this big seabag on my shoulder. The hammock, the seabag – it was 100 pounds probably. I only weighed about 118 pounds in those days. I was just a little scrawny dude. Here I was with this big bag going across there. I thought, my God, if I lose my balance and this bag swings over the side of the gangplank what am I going to do? I could see myself falling off the gangplank, bag and all, before I ever even stepped on the ship. No, I decided, I'll drop the seabag before I fall off and kill myself. It was a little scary but I made it across.

I saluted the officer of the deck; it's protocol.

I said, "Permission to come aboard, sir."

"Permission granted. I'll need your orders."

They took my orders and read them and logged them in the book and away I went. I entered a whole new world. I'd never been on a ship like that. You know, I really felt like I was somebody, that first day on the *Oklahoma*.

From audio recordings made on March 26, 2009 and June 15, 2009.

We Were Deck Seamen

While we were still in dry dock, they put all of us green seamen to work painting the sides and the bottom of the ship. We chipped the old paint off of it, wire brushed it, and then painted it with anti-corrosive paint. We called it red lead. That's actually what it was — red, lead paint, made mostly out of lead. We did that about a week or so.

One day they said, "We're pulling the chocks and getting ready to go to sea." The chocks were big wooden props that the boat rested on to keep it from rolling over. They started flooding the dry dock. We had to get all that water back in there and float the ship. I could hardly believe that big chunk of iron, that massive ship, would actually float. It didn't take too long to flood that dry dock and have the ship surrounded with water. There were tug boats that helped pull us out of the dock. Eventually, we came chugging toward the Golden Gate Bridge. I thought, boy, this is going to be something, passing through that Golden Gate and out into the world. For a kid who wanted to take a raft over the Rocky Mountains to get to the ocean, this was almost unreal to me. We went straight out to sea and headed to Pearl Harbor.

I was assigned to the third division. We were deck seamen. We took care of everything on the deck. The ship had a wooden deck. It was made out of teak, and we had to clean it every morning at five o'clock. We wet the deck down with salt water using the deck hose. Then we holystoned the deck. We had a sandstone rock that was just like a building block. And it had a hole in it. It was a round hole and you put a stick of a mop in it. We didn't call it a mop; we called it a swab. You put the swab stick in there and you holystoned the deck. There'd be four or five guys in a line. We all moved in unison and we scrubbed that sucker. Then we squeegeed it. My God, you could eat off of that deck; it was that clean. It was a beautiful old ship. Everything was clean and polished.

Then when we were all done cleaning the deck, we got a cup of coffee, our first cup of the day. The leading seaman would pour us a cup. These were round porcelain cups without handles. Usually we got one cup of coffee on deck, and then we went to breakfast down below. Our day to day routine settled in pretty quickly. We had plenty of work. Every morning, same, same.

We also had to take care of the floatplane that was on deck. This plane would take off and land on the water. It had two small pontoons on the outside and a big pontoon down the center. Whenever that plane would take off, we had to handle the lines to help get it ready. That was phenomenal for me to see something like that. This pilot would take that airplane off the ship about every day. Then when the plane came back for a landing, we had to help secure it. When he would land in the water, we swung out this big boom that had a wooden platform on it. We called it a sled. The sled trailed behind this boom. The pilot would taxi through the water and hook onto that sled. Then we pulled that airplane onto the sled. We had lines over our shoulders and they'd holler, "Run away with it." And that's what we did. Our legs were running as fast as hubcaps turning on a speeding car. We pulled the plane onto the sled and then we dropped a hook down to the airplane. Then we lifted the airplane up and swung it around up onto the deck and put it in its cradle. That pilot would come swaggering out of that airplane. We thought he was God himself. We idolized him, but we could never talk to him. We were just lowly deckhands and he was a rare breed of pilot.

It took us about a week to get to Hawaii. I had liberty and I could hardly believe it. Honolulu smelled like heaven. There were tons of food stalls everywhere. I never smelled or tasted food like that. Those smells gave me a ferocious appetite. You could eat yourself silly, trying all those different foods. It wasn't cheap, though. On twenty-one dollars a month pay, I had to watch my money.

There were bars. They weren't carding anybody in those days. I was just seventeen years old. But, as long as you had money to slap on the bar, they'd serve you.

There were brothels there, too, beautiful places, wide open to anyone. These were nicely kept places, clean and as respectable as places like those could get, I suppose. No phony baloney going on. Everything was up to date in Honolulu. So, we visited them, the houses of prostitution. We didn't get drunk and stagger up the stairs, that kind of stuff. But, I was there. I was young, and that was part of the game.

We left Hawaii and went back to Long Beach, and then we headed back to Pearl Harbor. That's when I started badgering the leading seaman.

From audio recordings made on March 26, 2009, October 9, 2009, and June 12, 2011.

Irvin in Hawaii, 1941

We're the Triangle Sailors

I was talking with the leading seaman there one morning when we were drinking our coffee after holystoning the deck. The leading seaman was pretty sharp. He was god to us green sailors.

I asked him, "How often does this battleship go to some of these foreign countries?"

He looked at me and he said, "You don't know do you?"

"No, I don't know," I said. "What don't I know?"

"We don't go anywhere. We're the triangle sailors. We start out in Oakland, we go to Hawaii, then to Long Beach. Then we start it over again. We don't go very far."

Man, he was right. I didn't know that.

He said, "You seem pretty intent on getting off of this ship."

"No, I don't want to get off. I just want to see more of this world than Pearl Harbor and Honolulu."

"I want to tell you something," he said. "I don't tell many guys this, but you go down to the bulletin board and you study that bulletin board every morning when you come off of duty here. Every now and then they'll put up a bulletin for people to go to the Asiatic Fleet, to the Philippines."

My eyes got big. "Really?"

"Really. You have to take some schooling. Every three or four months they put up openings in this mine school over at the submarine base in Pearl Harbor. It doesn't last long, two months or so and you're out."

If I took this schooling, then I could ask for a transfer to the Asiatic Fleet and I'd have this school on my record and they'd put me on a mine sweep. That would give me the ticket to get on a mine sweep stationed in the Philippines.

I said, "I'll do it." I'd get to see the Philippines. Maybe I'd even get to see China. I always wanted to go to China.

I went down there one morning and, lo and behold, there it stood, right on that bulletin board. Mine School – Pearl Harbor.

34

So, I went to the leading seaman. "Hey, they got a bulletin out for the mine school."

"Put in for it."

"What do I do?"

"Use a chit. I got 'em."

He showed me what the chits were. These were little documents, little requests to be transferred. I put in the chit. The leading seaman had to sign it. The division commander had to sign it. It got processed on through.

Meanwhile, we were out operating with the fleet on maneuvers. We were firing the big guns. That was the first time I heard a 14 inch gun go off. It was quite an experience. We also bumped into the *Arizona*. Our ship was supposed to zig and the *Arizona* was supposed to zag, but we zigged together and ran into each other. I felt the ship shutter. There was some damage, so we had to head back to Pearl to get it fixed.

Up at muster one morning, the chief said, "Hornkohl!"

"Yes, sir."

"Report down to the admin office. You've got your transfer to school."

So I went down there and, sure enough, I got temporary duty to the mine school. It was for two months, and then I was to report back to the *Oklahoma*. That was my key toward getting over to the Asiatic Fleet. This was November 1941.

From audio recordings made on March 26, 2009 and October 9, 2009.

A Beautiful Day to Be in Hawaii

I started mine school. I was still assigned to the *Oklahoma*, but I wasn't staying on it. I stayed at the mine school barracks right by the submarine base underneath the big diving tower. The diving tower was where they did training for deep sea diving. To me, those were beautiful barracks with neat rows of bunk beds. The barracks were right above the mess hall. It was a beautiful little mess hall.

There must have been fifty guys in the school. We were in class about eight hours a day. I made pretty good grades.

The *Oklahoma* was in the harbor part of the time, so I took a launch out on Sundays to see the guys a couple of times.

I worked in the bowling alley on the sub base at night. After supper I'd go over there. I was a duck pin man. Duck pins were about the size of a beer bottle. You had to set each one of them up after each ball. It was mainly officers doing the duck pin bowling. They'd shoot the ball down there and count their score, then I'd set up the pins. Every now and then those officers would shake loose and give me a tip. They'd give me a couple dollars. I thought it was a pretty good gig. This wasn't a regular job. I was just hanging out there setting pins.

I'd get enough money for the weekend and go to Honolulu. I'd drink a few beers, look at the girls and wander around. I was living in hog heaven. I thought to myself, going to mine school was an excellent decision.

We had the idea that war was imminent. We knew what was going on in Europe and the Japanese were getting fancy pants. But, you know, when you're seventeen years old you don't think anything is going to happen the next day. We didn't have training for war. In boot camp it was all, "hip, two, three, four" — marching and hand-washing our clothes and tying knots.

On December 7, 1941, I bailed out of bed pretty early. It was almost like any other day except it was a Sunday. I didn't have to go to work or to school. So I leisurely took a shower and got ready to go down to breakfast. I headed down the stairs and into the mess hall. Other guys were up. There were quite a few in the mess hall. After I got done eating about a quarter of eight, I started outside. I stood there looking around; it was a beautiful morning. No clouds, just a beautiful day to be in Hawaii.

Then all of a sudden I heard this machine gun fire going off. This plane came right over the barracks and let off quite a row of bullets. We just stood there in amazement at first. We couldn't believe this was happening. I looked up and saw those big red meatballs on the wings.

"Hell, that's Japs!"

From audio recordings made on October 9, 2009, October 10, 2009, and October 3, 2010.

Just Like a Swarm of Bees

All hell broke loose. Someone hollered, "Let's get to the armory."

So we all ran down to the armory. They had to cut the locks off to get the guns, and then they quickly passed out weapons. They gave us 30-06 rifles; the same gun I practiced shooting in boot camp. We grabbed belt line bandoliers with ammo on them. These 30-06s even had bayonets on them. It's a powerful rifle, but it's a bolt action. You can only get off one round at a time.

I ran back over to the dock because I saw these Japanese torpedo planes coming up the channel. I went to the edge of the dock and there were several submarines right there. The subs had machine guns on deck and they were cutting loose on these torpedo planes as they came over.

Those Japanese pilots, I could see their faces as they flew over me. They were that close, strafing with machine guns all over the place. The bullets were tearing up the grass fifty feet from us. Some of these planes had three guns on each wing. That's six machine guns going off at once; that's a pretty good pile of strafing. Of course, we were trying to knock them down. There were two or three other guys there with me who had rifles, too. I fired round after round as fast as I could. We popped a few holes in those planes with our rifles; we could hardly miss, they flew right over us. Planes were coming in pairs, just like a swarm of bees. Then the light bombers came after them.

Getting killed didn't even cross my mind. I wanted to kill the Japanese, though. I was so angry at what I was seeing, watching the battleships get hit. They had bombers coming over, but these weren't big bombers. These bombers came off of carriers and just had single engines. I saw the bomber that came down on the *Arizona*. The *Arizona* was pretty well intact up to this point. I watched that sucker fly over the *Arizona* and that bomb just dropped down. I thought it was going to go down the smoke stack. Some people say it landed forward of the smoke stack. I still think the bomb went down the stack. When it hit and blew up down below it must have been in the ammo locker, where the powder was. It looked like the whole ship just rose up out of the water and shook. Smoke everywhere. That bomb put the *Arizona* down and killed a lot of guys.

The stern of the *Pelias*, that's a submarine tender, was facing outboard, toward the channel. They had a 4"/50 caliber gun mounted on deck, which is a pretty heavy weapon. The *Pelias* cut loose with that 4"/50 and hit this torpedo plane right in the engine. The plane looked like it just stopped dead in midair. Then it dropped straight down into the water. Torpedo and all, thank goodness. He didn't have a chance to drop that torpedo.

Through the smoke I saw the *Oklahoma* lying there on her side, flipped practically upside down. I didn't see it happen, but I could see she was rolled over. I thought, my God, how many guys are in there? How many are trapped? They were in there trapped while I was out there on the dock. I knew there was no way to get back to the *Oklahoma*. I knew I was on my own. Every man for himself.

I was so focused the noise didn't bother me, even though there was enough racket from explosions and machine gun fire and airplanes to blow out my eardrums. There were fires burning and smoke was everywhere. I saw Hickham being hit. It was the biggest airbase in the area and she was getting hit hard. They were dropping bombs from 10,000 feet. I was firing at the planes flying over Hickham and this fellow said to me, "You're not going to hit anything."

"Maybe you're right, but it makes me feel better to keep firing at them." I got rid of quite a bit of ammunition. But I didn't run out. I had a whole belt full of ammunition. I stayed right there on the dock during the whole attack. We fired for a couple of hours, off and on.

Then word came out that the Japanese were invading, landing. The word just went up and down the line, so we put our bayonets on and got ready for combat. Of course, that didn't happen, thank goodness.

Finally, the planes stopped coming. There was nobody really in charge. People were just running around. Then I heard they wanted gun crews up high on this building near the diving tower. They had mounted machine guns up there on the top deck of this building. So, I went up there and stayed all day.

Everything was a disaster. From up on top of this building I could see everything that was going on all day. Motor launches were going around picking guys out of the water. The water was covered with oil. They brought some guys who were still alive back to the sub base. They all needed dry clothes. I went down and pulled clothes out of my locker and put them in the pile. Then I went back up on that building.

It was just mass confusion for awhile. We didn't know if the enemy was coming in again. The day finally wore into the evening. Motor launches were out there all night picking up guys, dead and alive, out of the water. We were there on top of that building through the night until the next morning. Everybody was awake. Nobody could sleep. Our nerves were wound up tighter than drums.

From audio recordings made on October 10, 2009 and October 11, 2009.

My Baptism in the Fire of War

The next morning word came along that they needed a working party to go out to the *Oklahoma*. Of course, I volunteered. There were maybe eight or ten of us that climbed into this launch. And I was still in whites, my dress whites, if you can imagine. We started out and I could see all the carnage. There were still bodies in different places, washed up here and there. People were out in launches, anything that would float, picking up bodies. There was smoke all over the place. The *Arizona* was still belching fumes.

We got out to the *Oklahoma* and we climbed up on the belly of the ship. We handled air lines to help these guys who were standing on the *Oklahoma*, trying to cut out the trapped men. They were using cutting torches and chipping guns. There was this big Hawaiian out there with muscles as big as suitcases. He worked in the shipyards. He was trying to cut these guys out. I'll never forget him, watching him work like a demon trying to save those guys. They had plans laid out, drawings of the ship. But, I don't know how much good those were. We went by sounds. We'd hear tapping – tap, tap, tap.

"Here's a sound over here!"

We'd rush over there and tap on the hull, and someone would tap back from inside. So, that's where we would start cutting. It was terrible; you could hear them down below. In some spots where we cut through, a blast of air would come out and the guys would holler, "Quit cutting, quit cutting!" As soon as the pressure was released through the hole, it let water come in. It was just horrendous. It tore my heart out.

I helped pull out three or four guys. I think, altogether, about thirty guys were pulled out from the ship. I did this all day, until evening. I don't remember being tired, even though I hadn't slept in about thirty-six hours. It was my birthday. My eighteenth birthday. I was so busy all day I don't think it even occurred to me that it was my birthday.

41

My whole world was upside down. In the evening they cut us loose and told us to go back to the barracks at the sub base. I don't think I'd eaten anything since the day before at breakfast.

I'll never in my life forget that day standing there on the *Oklahoma*. I'll carry it with me to my grave. It's stuck with me all these years. I can still hear those guys down there tapping. More than 400 guys died on the *Oklahoma*. It was heartbreaking. It was a lucky decision on my part to put in for the mine school and get off that ship.

I thought about the leading seaman who helped me get into mine school. He went down with the *Oklahoma*. It was heart-shaking. It took me a long time to learn to live with that. It took me twenty years, probably, before I could think about that time without it ripping me up. I'd wake up at night with bad dreams for years. I wasn't the only one. Others who survived felt the same way. I was a lucky survivor. I wondered, why me? Why was I spared? It's the way fate is. At times I felt guilty for surviving. I couldn't run around jumping for joy about surviving, not after all those other guys died. They weren't lucky like me.

I saw more action in three or four hours than some people did in the whole war. I saw enough killing to last a lifetime at Pearl Harbor. That was my baptism in the fire of war.

From audio recordings made on June 15, 2009, October 9, 2009, October 10, 2009, and November 30, 2010.

It Was Payback Time

For the next few days more rescue operations went on. They started cleaning up the harbor, trying to salvage what they could. I was out on the docks watching when they hauled that Japanese torpedo plane out of the water, the one the *Pelias* knocked out of the air right in front of me. That Japanese pilot was still sitting there in the cockpit with his hands on the controls.

I wrote a letter to my sister to tell her I was alive. It was just a little note, a speed letter, they called it. Well, it wasn't too speedy. It took about three weeks to get to her. My family knew I'd been assigned to the *Oklahoma*, but they didn't know I'd been transferred to mine school. They had no idea, for sure, whether I was alive or dead. They thought I was dead. I guess I could have sent them a telegram, but I'd never sent a telegram in my life. I was just a hick, really. A hick from the sticks. They were overjoyed when they got that letter.

The mine school started up again. It was awful strange going back to school, like everything was normal. But, we knew it wasn't normal. Nothing was normal ever again. I felt like I was in limbo. I had no ship, so I wasn't sure what was going to happen to me. Then before long, they assembled all of us from the mine school on the lawn at the sub base and they asked for volunteers.

"How many of you people want to go on submarines?"

"That's me!" I said.

Usually, they wouldn't let you on a submarine unless you went to sub school in New London, Connecticut. But, the war had started and they needed bodies. They stripped us down. We went through the line where they checked my heart, and they checked this and they checked that. Then they checked my eyesight. If you didn't have 20/20 vision you couldn't qualify for a submarine. It was pretty stiff requirements, even for that time when they needed us. I passed all of the physical tests. Then we had to take a written exam. If you had a low IQ, they wouldn't take you. I didn't finish in the top, but I didn't finish in the bottom, either. I passed all the tests, but I didn't know if I was accepted yet, and I still had to finish mine school.

Then I got the word; I was accepted. I was going to be a submariner. I was sent to the *Pelias*, a sub tender. A sub tender is a big ship that has about twelve subs assigned to it. The sub tender has a torpedo shop, a maintenance shop, supplies, just everything a sub needs to be fitted for a patrol. The *Pelias* had relief crews, too. So, when a submarine would come in off of patrol they would send relief crews off of the *Pelias* to go and take over the work on a sub that was in port. The sub's regular crew was sent to the Royal Hawaiian Hotel in Honolulu for some R and R.

A couple months after Pearl had been bombed, a submarine called the *Gudgeon* pulled into port after its first war patrol. We took over the *Gudgeon* as a relief crew. We started cleaning it up. Chipping stuff off the sides, cleaning, painting. Going down in the bilges to clean them out. Lots of different jobs. After two weeks in port, they were making up the crew for the *Gudgeon's* next patrol. I was hoping to get assigned to the *Gudgeon*. They had a good crew. Real professionals, career sailors. Some of them had been in the Navy six or eight years. Here I came along; I'd been in the Navy eight months. A real salt. But, they needed guys for some of the lower jobs that didn't need much training.

My name was on the list. I was ecstatic. I was really going to go to sea on a submarine. Nobody could have been any happier than I was. I wanted to get out there. It was payback time. I would have taken a rowboat with a .50 caliber machine gun mounted on the back and headed for Japan. To get back at the Japanese was pure joy. That's how a lot of us felt. We were Americans and we were attacked and a lot of our friends were killed at Pearl Harbor.

From audio recordings made on June 17, 2009 and October 10, 2009.

PART III
WORLD WAR II & SUBMARINES
1942 – 1945

"We were happy as hell to sink a Japanese ship. They got us at Pearl and it was their turn."

The Seas Were Just Boiling

Jake Hofer and I went aboard the *Gudgeon* together for the first time with our orders in hand. We were both survivors of Pearl Harbor. Ogden, this big stately chief of the boat, came up to me and said, "What's your name?"

"Irvin Hornkohl."

"Well, do you have Indian blood in you?"

I guess I must have looked the part. I was pretty tanned, anyway, and I had black hair. I don't know why he thought I had Indian blood. I wasn't going to disagree with him.

"That's probably true."

"From now on, you're not Irvin. You're Moose."

"Okay." That sounded good to me. If that was part of becoming a sub sailor, I was ready. He just pulled that name out of the air. He did that to all of the young guys who came on the boat. Next up was Jake Hofer. Actually, his name was William Hofer. The chief asked him the same thing.

Jake said, "My name is William Russell Hofer and I come from Iowa."

"Where the tall corn grows?"

"Yep."

"That's quite an impressive name, William Russell Hofer, but on the *Gudgeon,* you'll be known as Jake Hofer."

That's how we became Jake Hofer and Moose Hornkohl.

The *Gudgeon* had already been out on patrol. She went out toward Japan right after the war started. Ray Foster was a torpedoman on the *Gudgeon.* They sank a Japanese submarine on their first patrol, the first enemy ship sunk during the war. Ray wrote his daughter's name on the torpedo that sank that ship.

I was on the *Gudgeon* about a week while still in port, and then we headed out to sea. It's close living on a submarine. You take about seventy men and jam them into a living space of about 280 feet by 24 feet, that's close. And overhead with all the piping and valves, I had to learn to dodge that stuff. On the first patrol, I knocked myself around a few times, slamming my head into those pipes. After I learned where the valves were, I instinctively ducked without even thinking about it.

A submarine has different stations, like the after torpedo room and the forward torpedo room. They're all hooked up on this phone line. I was a phone talker in the control room. The control room was where they did all the business, taking care of the ship, and I had to receive all of these messages. So, I was a phone talker, getting messages from around the sub on the phone line, and sending out messages from the control room. I was great until we got to sea.

I was seasick. I was so seasick I ran around with a bucket. As soon as we dove in the morning, I was fine. We'd come up at night, though, and those six days going to Midway Island were rough. The seas were just boiling all the time. On the surface the sub would go up and down and when the sub went down my stomach went with it. We had stabilizers on each side, so rolling wasn't too bad. But, when the sub was pitching up and down, that got me in trouble.

They said, "You can't be a phone talker running around with that bucket."

So, they talked to old Brock. He was the ship's cook. Big, bald-headed fellow. He was probably pretty close to retirement. He was one *magnifico* cook.

They said, "Brock, you need a mess cook don't you?"

"Yeah. I need a good one."

They asked me, "Are you a good mess cook?"

"Well, I've never mess cooked."

Brock said, "You'll do all right. Just do what I tell you."

"I'll do it. Anything you say."

"You got to get up at four o'clock every morning."

"Four o'clock?"

"Four o'clock."

I hated to get pulled off of my job, but I could see they couldn't handle a phone talker running around with a bucket. So, I went to work for Brock.

He said, "See those potatoes? I need a big pan full of them for tonight."

"Okay, Brock." I went to peeling.

I was a hell of a mess cook. I had never been a cook before, but I knew I could do it. I was pretty agile in those days. I could do most jobs. I didn't go to high school. I had to work. A lot of the other guys on the sub had been to high school, except me. So, working, doing manual labor, just came natural to me. I could handle whatever job they gave me. That's what kept me on the boat. I was kind of a weak link there at first on the phone lines, which was an important job. They couldn't keep me on it because of the seasickness. I thought, oh boy, when we get to Midway they're going to transfer me. So, I just did the best job I could in the mess and didn't worry about it.

I enjoyed the kitchen work. I really did. We had four tables with three men sitting on each side. I set the plates out and the silverware. They liked the tables to look halfway decent. We had cups, but no glassware. After I got all the tables set, I would stand by the window to the kitchen and Brock would say, "Here's this for table one." It'd be a big platter of steaks and I'd take it out there and set it down and rush back and get another platter. I was pretty speedy. We had about sixty-two people on the sub. They'd come through in three sections. Three times a day. When the first section finished, I had to clean up the dishes. Cleaning up after twenty-four people at a time. That was a lot of dishes. We had two big sinks, deep double sinks. I had to clean the cook's stuff, too, the pots and the pans. It wasn't an easy job, but it was a beautiful job, in a way. It kept me busy and I actually got to know people.

Brock did most of the cooking. I was his hired hand. I did everything he told me. "Wash the dishes, wash the pots. Go down in the freezer and get the meat." We had big pork roasts and beef roasts. Some days we'd have steak, some days, steak and eggs. And maybe one day on the patrol we'd get steak and lobster together. Man, we were living high on the hog.

48

When we got to Midway after that first week, I figured they were going to transfer me. I thought, well, if I get transferred off at Midway, I'll go on a relief crew and catch another submarine and I'll be a few days wiser. We got to Midway and I didn't see anybody signing my ticket off the boat. Nobody ever said anything to me. I was glad when we were throwing off the lines leaving Midway. I was still aboard the *Gudgeon*. I wanted to be a sub sailor in the worst way. The seasickness was gone. Just about six days was all I had it. I never got seasick again on submarines.

I worked as a mess cook that whole first patrol, about two months, until we pulled into Pearl again. The crew made up a kitty for me. I never dreamed that was going to happen. They took up a kitty and gave me tips.

The chief of the boat came by and said, "You were a good mess cook," and he gave me the money. It was less than fifty dollars, but that was still a lot of money to me.

On that first patrol we sank two ships; we had depth charges and we had some aerial bombs dropped on us, too. I got it all on that first patrol. I wasn't sure that I had bargained for that much excitement. But, I took to it all okay. I wasn't afraid, but I sure was concerned. You want to live, of course, but the thought of dying wasn't on my mind the whole time.

I never even went on deck that first patrol. I'd only been in the Navy less than a year. I was still a raw recruit. That first patrol was my indoctrination into submarines, and I decided I was going to be all right. I knew I was cut out for this duty.

From audio recordings made on June 17, 2009, October 10, 2009, November 30, 2010, and January 25, 2011.

Blow Up the Enemy

On my first patrol on the Gudgeon, I was the mess cook. But, I knew I wanted to strike for a torpedoman. You couldn't just land on a submarine and expect to be a salty seaman. You had to work into your rate. So, I'd go up to the torpedo room to help them routine fish. That's what we called it. To routine a torpedo you pulled it out of the tube and charged it with air, making sure you had 3,000 pounds in the flask. There's an igniter that went into the chamber that ignited the fire in the torpedo. So, you'd disconnect the igniter and reconnect it, just testing it. You had to check all of these things to make sure everything was ready to fire. We'd routine torpedoes about every week on patrol. It gave me a good chance to work in the torpedo room and let the guys get to know me.

In the meantime, I was trying to qualify. In order to stay on the submarine, you had to qualify. You had to know every valve on the boat. You had to know what everything did, how to turn it off and on, how to operate every little thing. There were jillions of things you had to learn. You might think, well, this is somebody else's job. That wasn't the way on the submarines, though; you had to know everybody's job. I had to study hard.

When it finally came to qualifying day, an officer would go through the sub with you and you had to show him what every valve did; you had to trace all of the air lines; you had to know how to take on water, and how to make water. You had to put the four engines on line and take them off; you had to work the electrical switch boards. You had to know everything about the torpedo tubes, how to make a torpedo ready, how to fire it. I was a busy, busy fellow learning all this. If you couldn't hack it, then they would transfer you off the ship. When it came time for me to qualify, I was fairly confident. But, I was a little worried about starting the engines. After I practiced it a couple of times, I could do it all right. To say that I wasn't nervous about qualifying would be a fib, but when the inspection time came, I qualified.

On my second patrol on the Gudgeon, I was a striker in the after torpedo room. That means I planned to work into becoming a torpedoman. I was like an apprentice under this fellow named Wixted. He was a second class torpedoman. He was a real salty sailor. He had his own bunk in the after torpedo room. I thought, my God, if I ever get a bunk in the torpedo room, I'll be in hog heaven. I loved the torpedo room.

Wixted was a good teacher. He'd say, "Don't touch that valve!" I couldn't touch anything until I was trained. When you're a striker, they don't turn you loose on anything. You're under the watchful eye of the other torpedomen.

We had four tubes in the after room, six tubes in the forward torpedo room. When we left port on a new patrol, we had twenty-four torpedoes aboard. Six in the forward tubes, four in the after tubes, and fourteen on the skids. The skids were these cradles that held the extra torpedoes. You really had to be on the ball in that torpedo room. If you screwed up, you could fire a torpedo through the door. There were usually three guys in the torpedo room for battle stations. Sometimes a fourth guy would be there to help.

We always had torpedoes in the tubes ready to fire whenever we spotted the enemy. You had to follow a sequence of events to fire that torpedo. The first thing we did was flood the tubes with water to equalize the pressure with the outside pressure of the seawater. There were vents that vented off each torpedo tube. You had to open the vents to bring the water in to flood the tubes. After we flooded the tubes and the pressure was equalized, then you opened the outer door of the torpedo tube by cranking it open. We didn't have hydraulic outer door openers on the *Gudgeon*. We had to crank the doors open. There was a big brass cranker, like the cranks on old cars, only twice as big. Wixted was an ace at opening those doors. I loved to watch him. I watched everything he did.

On battle stations, one man was between the tubes setting the depth of the torpedo. You had to set the depth for each torpedo by hand. The torpedoes had a depth setter built into them. There was a spindle built into the torpedo and you turned that to set the depth; it could have been eight feet or ten feet, whatever the skipper wanted.

The guys up in the conning tower set the angle of the torpedo. We had a mechanical computer that would set the angle. If something went wrong up there, we had to set that angle by hand.

There was a second guy between the tubes; he was the interlock man. You couldn't touch the interlocks until you had a lot of experience. Interlocks were mechanical safety devices on the tubes that would keep you from getting things out of sequence. Sort of like a safety mechanism on a gun. The interlock man also wore headphones that were connected to the conning tower. He could hear what was going on up there and knew which torpedo was going to fire. He might hear "Fire one!" He'd hold his hand up to torpedo one, and if it fired electronically, then that was it. The torpedo would shoot out of there and he'd throw that lock down to clear the tube and close the doors after it had fired. But, sometimes the electrical systems would get grounded out and didn't work. Then you had to push a button to send that torpedo off. I hand-fired torpedoes several times.

On my second patrol I finally got the chance to open the outer doors.

"Do what I do," Wixted said. That wasn't an easy job getting those outer doors open. I felt like I really was on the firing line. I felt like I was a part of the battle.

We'd usually fire three torpedoes at a time. We'd fire a spread of three and hope that one of them would catch the ship. One would go to the left, then another would go down the throat, that's what we called it, and another would go more to the right. Kind of like a fan. The enemy would have to do a bunch of dodging to get away from a spread. Of course, early on we had a bunch of dud torpedoes. The exploders wouldn't go off. We could hear them hitting the ship, but they wouldn't explode. Eventually, they got that worked out.

Later in the war when I was on the *Sealion II*, I was the interlock man, a second class torpedoman. By that time, torpedoes were getting more sophisticated. We had some little torpedoes that had acoustic heads on them. We'd fire one of those suckers and they would seek out the sound of the screws on the enemy's ship. That's what we called a ship's propeller, the screws. These little torpedoes would blow his screws off and then we'd come back and sink him. That's what we were out there for, blow up the enemy.

You could hear the torpedoes hitting those ships. We'd hear the impact and sometimes we'd even hear the detonator go off, if we were close enough to the target. Sound in water travels a terrific distance. When we hit the target and that ship blew up, we'd cheer and holler, "We got those bastards!" We'd cut loose, for sure. We were happy as hell to sink a Japanese ship. They got us at Pearl and it was their turn. That was clear in my mind. I never felt remorse when we sank a ship. That just wasn't in my vocabulary. I think most sub sailors felt the same way.

From audio recordings made on June 17, 2009, October 9, 2009, October 10, 2009, November 30, 2010, and February 17, 2011.

We Could Hear Him Coming for Us

A depth charge is something that's hard to describe. It's about 300 pounds of high explosives in a barrel, about the size of a thirty gallon trash can. They had igniters in them and when they reached a certain depth, that's when they exploded. They could set the depth for 100 feet, 200 feet, 300 feet. As soon as it went to that depth, the igniter would go off.

The submarine would be hiding out underwater and the enemy would be up there trying to figure out where we were. If they thought they were close to us, they'd drop a depth charge. I could hear those barrels hit the water with a big splash. I waited and waited and then, bingo, I heard that detonator go off, and then came the big explosion. It made the hair on the back of my neck stand out.

Some of the depth charges were very close and shook the boat something terrible. Those destroyers would just shower us with depth charges. They were trying to pop holes in us. That's the name of the game for killing a submarine – blow a hole in the side.

Sometimes, the depth charges would just shake the dickens out of me. They would blow light bulbs out, too. Depth charges have been known to break a man's ankles from the force of being knocked off his feet. That's why they made all of us go to bed during depth charge attacks. Everybody who wasn't on watch would get in their sacks and take it as it came. I would rather be on the wheel or on the bow planes or on the stern planes doing something real physical during a depth charge attack, than just lying there. I did a lot of thinking lying in my sack while being bombed. It was terrifying at times.

When the enemy was out there hunting for the sub, we rigged for silent running. Everything was shut off. We shut off the air conditioner; we shut off the power pumps. We had power pumps to hydraulically turn the rudder and the bow planes and the stern planes. When we shut everything off, the bow planesman and the stern planesman, who were in charge of trying to keep that boat level, had to operate by hand. The diving officer would tell them how many degrees down bubble and how many degrees up. Sometimes, the helmsman, who was steering the ship, really had to crank that wheel to maintain a course. He had to pump that sucker to keep the rudder answering what the old man said. If he hollered out, "Helmsman, give me course 360," and if that was way on the other end, he really had to pump.

It seemed like it'd take us an hour to make a turn when we were hand pumping. Finally, the helmsman just crapped out. The air was hot, 120 degrees, and somebody else had to take over real quick. Another guy took over and pumped for awhile, and when he was about to knock out, the helmsman would go back on the wheel.

When we ran silent, nothing, no sound, could come out of the submarine except the screws. You had to maintain some kind of way, which means you're moving. You had to maintain way or the sub would sink. Finally, when we were silent running, everything just ran out. We ran out of air and out of battery power.

The enemy would shut everything off, too, while they were pinging with this electronic sound wave going through the water.

Boing. Boing. Boing.

I could hear the pings real clearly. They could send out those pings very rapidly. That was hair-raising to listen to. Everyone was real tense because we knew they were looking for us. When that ping bounced off the sub, it sounded kind of like throwing a baseball and hitting a wall. It told them exactly where we were and how deep. Man, then he could just come right for us. We could hear their screws start up. We didn't need sound gear to hear that destroyer coming after us. We knew there was going to be a big bang when they dropped those depth charges.

Of course, we tried to get away from that guy up there. We'd try to sneak out and get as far from him as we could. He would chase us and every time he heard a screw, he was after us. We could hear him coming for us. I'd wonder, well, how close is it going to be this time?

When I wasn't on watch, lying there in my bunk during a depth charge attack, I wondered, what am I gonna do when the water comes in? I asked myself, how am I gonna die? Am I gonna take a big gulp? Am I gonna just lie there? If he blew a hole in the side, there'd be tons of water on me in a matter of a minute. I used to think about that. How was I gonna die? I couldn't do anything about it. I just hoped it was quick. I had to relax and take it.

From audio recordings made on October 9, 2009, October 10, 2009, February 20, 2010, June 21, 2010, and November 30, 2010.

I Was the Captain of That Rubber Boat

We were getting ready to go off a patrol and head down to Freemantle, Australia. We had to go through the Lombok Strait off the island of Bali. It's a big channel through there; it's very swift.

I used to hang out in the radio shack when I could. I'd stick my nose in there and ask the radioman, "Anything new? What are we doing?" Well, this time something was stewing.

"They got something hot up in the wardroom," he said. "They're deciphering it now."

I thought, boy, I'll just hang around the control room and find out what it is.

This message said that we had to pick up these guys on the island of Timor. They were commandos, Australian commandos. The Nippies had chased them all the way across the island and the commandos had radioed out, "You got to get us or we'll be annihilated." They'd been without food and had been fighting all the way across the island. The Nippies were right back in the hills behind them. We knew that the Japs wouldn't leave any survivors. Once the Nippies got you, your head would come off.

So, we went up there to rescue these commandos. We pulled into the cove that night and made preparations for getting crews to go across to the island. It was about a mile to the beach from the sub. I was up on deck with the head deckhand helping to pull out these rubber boats. Mr. Dornin was the executive officer in charge of this operation. I volunteered to take a boat over. He didn't ask for volunteers. I just wanted to go.

I said, "I know all about boats." I didn't tell him that me and Jack McFee nearly drowned in the frog pond.

"I don't know, Moose. Can you handle it?"

"Just put me in there and I'll do the job."

"Well, okay, Moose. You're one."

Then he picked a couple others. Ray Foster and Pappy Low. We called him Pappy because he was thirty-two years old, an older guy. The plan was to take the boats over and load them up with the commandos. The problem was getting the darn boats over there. It was nighttime and all we had was a flashlight. The commandos on the beach gave us one burp of light and then we'd answer back with one burp. Then we just kept paddling.

We did great paddling over there, but then as soon as we got close to the beach all dickens broke out. The waves were high. The waves knocked us around as we tried to land on the beach. The waves would shoot us back and then pull us forward real fast. We didn't want to kill ourselves, or wreck our boats crashing onto the beach. We'd paddle backwards real hard, trying not to ride the top of the wave. Finally, we made it through and landed the boats on the beach.

The commandos were there along with some natives who were being trained to fight the Japanese. Those commandos were real tough dudes. But they didn't look very tough when we got over there. Just skin and bones. We started loading them. The other guys ended up with English-speaking people in their boats. I ended up with all the natives. I got these guys and I couldn't communicate with them. I think I had six in my boat. We were loaded too heavy. They kept jumping in. But, I couldn't throw them out; I didn't have the heart to tell any of them they couldn't go. But, and this is the real sad part, some of the natives had wives there, too. We couldn't take their wives. I wanted to get them all off that island, but we didn't have enough boats. The Nippies were right back on the side of the hill coming down. There was some firing going on. It was real imperative to get out of there. Nobody likes getting your head chopped off. That was the fate we'd have if we hung around that beach. I had a .45 on me but I doubt that .45 would have shot anybody because it was soaking wet.

We must have spent an hour fighting that surf trying to get going. Lord knows how I did it. We were washed ashore three or four times. The surf would just upend the boat and dump us all out into the water. So, I would get that boat flopped down again and gather them up. We were all soaking wet and pretty tired.

This last time I kept telling them to shovel the water out. We needed something that would hold water, so the natives took my shoes and they were bailing with those. And it helped. If I'd have hit the beach again, I would have been out there barefooted as heck. Anyway, we finally made one of the crests, and we slid down the backside of the wave and we moved out. I paddled and they talked amongst themselves. They were speaking Portuguese. I was raised around a lot of Hispanics so I knew some Spanish. I could pick out from the Portuguese similar words to Spanish. It helped me understand them a little.

There weren't any boats around coming back with me. The others were ahead of us. It was me, all alone. I had six non-English-speaking guys. I was trying with gestures, anything I could think of, to communicate while still paddling that boat. Every once in awhile, I'd get a blink of light from the sub. I'd try to head for it. That night was so dark you couldn't see your hand in front of your face. It's a real wonder I found that sub. I was pooped. But when you're exhausted, it seems like you suck in another five yards of strength. Sometimes the natives would get their hands out and try to paddle, but I couldn't always be sure I was going the right direction. It was hard for me to keep heading for that last light that I saw. It seemed like it would take an eternity to see that light again. And I couldn't tell them to look for the light. So, it was just me. I was the captain of that rubber boat.

It was starting to get light. Time goes pretty fast when you're trying to pull something like that off. It was starting to break dawn and I heard the engines start up. And I thought, oh Christ, here I go. They're gonna leave without us. The old man had said, "If you're not back when it gets light, we're going to go because they'll knock us out of the water." He had the whole ship's crew to think about. If it came down to the crew and one or two guys out in the water, he was going to leave the guys. And, I knew it would be me who was left behind. I managed to get close enough and could see the outline of the sub.

"I'm coming! I'm coming! Don't leave yet!"

Finally, we pulled up alongside the sub. We got those fellows out, and then we pulled the rubber boat up and deflated it.

Mr. Dornin said, "How do you feel, Moose?"

"Pooped."

The other boats had made it back already. It wasn't long and we headed out.

That whole episode was a nice phase of my life. It really was. The other guys were all kidding me. "Where's your crew, Moose?" I was quite a guy for awhile. They were nicely teasing me. There wasn't anything obnoxious. I appreciate the nice things they said about me. I was awarded the Navy and Marine Corps medal for heroic conduct. That was a proud moment for me. I gave it my all. I wasn't a bit scared to go to that island. I should have been terrified, but I wasn't. I could have given my life on that beach. But I didn't think of it that way. I told Pappy on that night when we were going across to the beach, "Pappy, I feel like I'm finally doing something for my country." Here I'd been in half a war already. Although, I'll admit, when I was the last guy left on that island trying to get back to the boat, I was wondering if patriotism was all it was cracked up to be. But, in the end, I knew it was the right thing to do and I was proud to do it. That's how most Americans were then.

From audio recordings made on October 10, 2009 and September 25, 2011.

We're All Going to Be Dead, Anyway

Everybody was trained for two or three jobs. On the *Gudgeon* when we surface-battled somebody, I was the number three loader on that old 3"/50 caliber gun that we had. To fire that big gun you needed a gunner and a sight-setter, then there's a loader, and a hot shellman, then me. I was third in line. If one of those guys got knocked out, killed or injured, then I'd move on up to the next position.

One night we went into this place called Surabaya in the Java Sea. We were following what looked like an ocean patrol craft. The skipper said, "Battle stations surface. We'll take him with the deck gun."

So, we went to battle stations surface. That meant we were riding on the surface. We were following this ship trying to catch him. I was right on the deck standing in line to help load the 3"/50. We got up close to this guy and all of a sudden he turned on us and fired. Then everything started going bad. We realized this was a destroyer and he could take us out. We never dreamed it was a destroyer. It was a small-sized ship for a destroyer, but still loaded with weapons that could do us in.

He swung around and that put his bow right on us and he fired a couple rounds. Luckily they didn't hit us. They were awfully close. I could see the shells bursting in the water. About this time in the after torpedo room they'd made the after tubes ready, four of them. They were setting them up to fire. Ducky Drake fired the four torpedoes and the spread went out and that destroyer was trying to dodge them. He got away from them, but that slowed him down and gave us more time. So, we were able to get another few hundred yards ahead of him.

Then we started firing our 3"/50 and we hit him right in his big deck gun and knocked it out. Man, that was a lucky hit. That saved us. We got a few more rounds fired at him and, in the meantime, we were trying to turn and head out. We'd been chasing this guy about two hours and the water

61

was too shallow to dive. The water under us was only about fifty or sixty feet, so we couldn't dive. He had been leading us there. He could have turned at any time and come back at us. He knew where that shallow water was. The only thing left was to keep firing at this dude, which we did. We tried to make for the open sea. He was machine-gunning us and I could see the bursts of fire coming from him.

Our skipper, Wild Bill Post, called down to the engine room and he said, "Maneuvering, I want everything you can give me on those engines."

"We're giving you everything now, Skipper."

"I don't care. Give us some more."

"If I give you any more, we're liable to blow the engines."

"It won't make any difference if we blow the engines or not. We're all going to be dead, anyway, if this guy gets us."

They boosted those engines as much as they could. In the meantime, we were still firing that 3"/50, popping shells in there. We could get the gun loaded and fired every five or ten seconds. It was chaos with all the gunfire coming at us. We were trained, though, and we kept our cool. I was standing there ready to pop that shell into the next guy's hands. It takes a whole crew to battle the enemy. I concentrated on doing my job, getting those shells up to the gunners. I didn't have time to be scared. I couldn't panic.

Finally, they said, "Secure the gun crew. Clear the decks." So we all scrambled to get down the hatch and I had a shell in my hands. They're pretty heavy, thirty or thirty-five pounds. I had this big shell and I came down trying to maintain a little stability. George Seiler was over there grabbing the ammunition, and I dropped the shell, which could have been a big problem. But, we got everything stowed and we got out of there alive.

We finally got out far enough and deep enough so we could dive. He came over with depth charges. But he missed us. That was a pretty hectic night.

From audio recordings made on October 9, 2009 and April 13, 2010.

You'll Get No Beer Here

Officers are off limits. You don't talk back to them. I learned that the hard way. After my sixth patrol on the *Gudgeon*, we pulled into Freemantle, Australia. We got two weeks leave. When we came into port, everybody got a ticket for a case of beer. There was a little building there in town designated as a beer drop. It was like a little store. You'd take your ticket there and they'd give you your beer.

We all got our seabags and off we went to the Ocean Beach Hotel in Perth. I didn't stop to get my beer, though. I thought, I'll go and get it tomorrow. I don't know what I did with that ticket, but I lost it. I probably left it on the boat. I could have taken a taxi back to the boat and looked for it. But, I thought, I'll go to the beer drop and explain that I lost the ticket. This was early evening and I'd already had a few beers, but I wasn't drunk. I went into the beer shack.

"I'm from the *Gudgeon*. My name is Hornkohl. I'm on your list there, but I haven't got my ticket for the beer."

That officer stood there looking at me, and there were two or three guys from the shore patrol there, too, guarding all that beer. "You'll get no beer here without your ticket."

"It's back on the sub."

"If you don't have a ticket, you're not getting any beer."

"What the hell?" I used a few foul words there under my breath. "We've just made a patrol run and it was rough. I just want my case of beer and I'll get out of here. I don't know what happened to my ticket. I left it on the boat, probably. My name's right there on your list."

He was getting hot, I could tell. "You sailors come in here and want your beer," he said. "Nobody comes in here and grabs beer without proper authorization."

"That's just like you guys," I said. "You lay around here in port instead of being out there fighting the war. You non-combatant son of a bitch."

Then I left. I could hear them grumbling and getting all worked up when I went outside. I probably could have calmed them down, if I'd kept my head. I strolled on down the street and went to a couple hotel bars. They were beautiful. You could go in there and order a drink and sit down at a table. Then I went on outside and walked down Hay Street. Australians called it "Eye" street. I saw Campy, a sailor I knew.

"Hey, Moose," he called. "Moose, they're looking for you."

"Who's looking for me?"

"The shore patrol. They want you bad. What'd you do?"

"You don't want to know."

"You probably better hide out for awhile. We're going down to a party in another town. You want to come?"

"No. I'll just weather this storm and see how this turns out. I'm not worried about the shore patrol."

Campy left and I hung around on the street, talking with some Aussie soldiers. I loved talking with them. We Americans would see these Aussies and we'd salute one another and talk about what wonderful fighters we were. Then here came the shore patrol.

They said, "Are you Hornkohl?"

"Yeah."

I thought, oh boy, this is getting serious. I didn't strike an officer. But I did use some foul language. Nobody had been hurt, but that didn't matter to them. I didn't put up a fight. I thought they'd hold onto me for a day or two and then let me finish my leave and get back to the *Gudgeon*.

They took me to the local jail, if you want to call it a jail. It was a tremendous building. It was an old prison, where the Australians had held the really bad guys. The Navy had taken over the whole building. They kicked me into a cell. It wasn't really a cell; it was actually a cement hole. Like a dungeon. There was hay on the floor, straw. No bed. No windows. You couldn't stand up in there. You almost had to crawl into the darn thing. It was about four feet by six feet. If you can imagine a sailor being thrown in something like that after he'd been on all these war patrols. They shouldn't have put me in there. But, in those days, you didn't have any rights.

They kept me in this awful place for three days. Nobody told me what was going on. This officer from the beer shack was a real bad ass. He was rotten. Maybe what I'd said to him hit too close to home. Maybe he knew it was true. Anyway, he wrote up all of these charges. He said I was unruly and drunk. I wasn't drunk. He said I was abusive and threatening. How could I be threatening to him? He had two or three shore patrol guys in there with him who could have jumped on me and busted my skull with their clubs.

Finally, they took me to the *Pelias*, the sub tender that was anchored at Freemantle. I didn't know what was going on. There was no hearing or anything like that. Apparently, they had to deal with all of these charges that this officer wrote up, one way or another. You couldn't say what I said to that officer and get away with it. I could have had a deck court martial, a summary court martial, or a general court martial. If it got to a general court martial, they could have taken me out and shot me. A deck court martial was the lowest of the courts martial. They could restrict you to the ship. That's what ended up happening to me. They realized I was a pretty proficient sailor. My background was pretty heavy duty. I was a combat sailor. It wouldn't do anybody any good to take me out and shoot me.

They took me off the *Gudgeon* and put me in the seventh division. They assigned me to the torpedo shop on the *Pelias*. I never saw the *Gudgeon* again. It broke my heart to leave the *Gudgeon*. I loved that ship. A year later, I was on the *Sealion* and I heard that the *Gudgeon* was lost. I felt terrible. I knew a lot of guys who were still on the *Gudgeon*. At that time, we had no idea what happened to it. Probably sunk by the Japanese. I was really hurt by that news. I moped around for a few weeks. Here I was alive on the *Sealion*, and those guys were dead at the bottom of the ocean. It was fate, I guess.

From audio recordings made on October 3, 2010 and January 25, 2011.

He Was No Choir Boy

I stayed on the *Pelias* in Freemantle for about three months. This was in 1943. I worked in the torpedo shop. I tore the torpedoes down and put them back together. It was all maintenance work. It was actually good for me because I hadn't been to submarine school, so in the torpedo shop I learned a lot more about how the torpedoes operated. I learned everything I could. Later, I got to go out on the subs that came into port and I did maintenance on them.

On the *Pelias*, we made a trip up to Exmouth Gulf, up north of Freemantle. The night that we took off, it was black as pitch. We backed out and worked our way out of the harbor with tugs, and we started up the coast. It took us about two days to get up there and tie up in the harbor. Exmouth Gulf was a good safe haven.

Well, I say it was safe enough, but Japanese bombers could get there pretty easily. About every night for two or three weeks the Japanese came over and bombed us. They never hit us. They were pretty close, though. There was one guy that came over every night. I could tell by listening to his engines. They were out of sync. His props weren't turning at the same rpm. I was on watch a couple times when they came over. We never fired at them; it was night and they were so high we couldn't see them. But, they could see us. Finally, the command got shaky and they decided to get the *Pelias* out of there. So we went back to Freemantle.

Meanwhile, one of my submarine buddies Eddie Ellis, was on the *Pelias*, too. I can tell this story about him now. He died a long time ago. Anyway, while we were in Freemantle, Eddie and I went with these two young ladies. Molly was the lady I went with and Eddie went with a gal named May. Eddie was head over heels in love with May. Something went wrong, I don't know where, but Eddie got gonorrhea.

He said to me, "Moose, I've just got to get over and see May."

"You can't. You're on restriction." They restricted guys to the ship when they got venereal diseases. Conduct unbecoming a sailor, that sort of thing.

"All you got to do, Moose, is stand up for me in line when they're passing out the medicine."

"I don't know about that, Eddie. I don't think I can pull that off."

"Oh, you can do it. Do this for me and we'll forever be buddies."

"Okay."

So, he left the ship and when they called Eddie's name at muster to come and get his medicine I shouted out "Here, sir!" Then I had to take his pills. It was Sulfathiazole.

Eddie was gone for a few days. He was only supposed to be gone one night. That darn medicine started turning my eyes yellow. I finally found Eddie and told him to get his butt back to the ship. I was afraid that if they found out what I was doing, I was going to really be in trouble, especially after that beer incident with the officer.

Eddie came back and they found out somehow that he'd been gone. I don't know what the formal charges were, but he got ten days of what we called piss and punk. That's bread and water in the brig on the *Pelias*. For some reason, I didn't get in trouble for the whole deal. I was damn lucky there. As it turns out, I was on watch every three days as a brig guard while Eddie was in there. So, every three days he'd get a big sandwich that I'd sneak down to him.

Eddie got married when he came back to the States and led a good life. A few years later, after the war, I served with Eddie on another sub. His wife must have heard some of these stories. She hated me with a passion. She must have thought I was a bad influence on him. But, I couldn't be a bad influence on Ellis. He'd already been influenced by a load of other guys before he ever met me. He was no choir boy. Most of us weren't.

From an audio recording made on February 17, 2011.

We'll Tear Up the Japanese Together

While I was still assigned to the *Pelias*, the *Grayling* came into Freemantle. My old buddy Campy was on the *Grayling*. I went over to the sub and found Campy sitting on his bunk down in the torpedo room.

"Are you getting ready to go out?" I asked.

"Yep, it won't be long. We just have to finish loading our supplies, and then we're out of here."

"I sure would like to catch this boat and go with you." I was ready to get back to sea. I was done with my restrictions from that beer incident.

"Moose," Campy said, "I'll talk to the exec and see if we've got room for you aboard. We'll tear up the Japanese together on this sub."

So, Campy went and talked to the executive officer. The exec said, "Yeah, we can take him aboard. Tell him to get his orders." The exec wrote the request and I dashed over to personnel and they said, "Okay, get your seabag and go on down to the *Grayling*. We'll start on your orders."

It didn't take me half an hour to get my seabag packed and down on the deck of the *Grayling*. Then I ran back to the personnel office. Someone came up to me and said, "No, you can't go. You haven't finished your restriction, yet."

"My God, I thought that was over."

"Nope, you've still got some time left on your restriction."

So they cancelled the orders. I was devastated. I missed the *Grayling* by just a hair's breadth. I went back and got my bag off the boat and stood there moping on the dock. I can still see Campy and some other guys standing there on the deck as they pulled away. I never saw those guys again. They never came back. They were sunk on that patrol. It was like a bad dream. It was a matter of luck for me, I guess.

From an audio recording made on January 25, 2011.

They Popped Me Right in There

I was finally done with my restriction on the *Pelias*. I was anxious to catch a sub. I was a combat sailor and I wanted to get back out there. I went up to the personnel office about every day, pestering them.

"Anything for me, yet?"

I wouldn't let them forget me. Finally, the *Gar* came into port and she was short a second class torpedoman. I fit the bill. They popped me right in there. I was happy. I knew a few guys on the *Gar*. Submarine sailors are a pretty tight group. I fit right in. No problems at all. I worked in the forward torpedo room.

We went out on patrol and sank two or three ships. But, we hit something out in the water; they said it was a big log. Whatever we hit messed up one of the screws. A couple of the blades were bent. Whenever it would rotate, it made tons of noise. Thump, thump, thump. You can't have that kind of noise when you're running silent; the enemy would pick us right up.

We went to Pearl Harbor and they pulled the boat up into dry dock to fix that propeller. So, they gave us leave and asked me if I'd like to get on a brand new submarine. New construction is what they called it. I said that would be great. I guess they figured since I had survived seven war patrols, which was actually pretty rare, that I deserved to get new construction for my next assignment.

So, I got thirty days leave and I went home to Colorado. My first time home in over two years. My dad was overjoyed to see me, his wayward son. Of course, I told my dad stories about what I'd seen and been through. To him, it was almost like something out of a book. I was leading a life that he could hardly imagine. Dad let me borrow his car, an old '31 Oldsmobile, to go down to Denver.

I told him, "Pop, I might not be back for a few days. I'm used to going out and being on my own."

"Whatever you want," he said. "You're grown up now."

I went down to Denver to this nightclub on Santa Fe Street. They served minors. As long as you could waddle up to the bar, they'd serve you. I went into the club and there was this pretty girl sitting in a booth over in the corner with her mother. I was in my dress blues, looking pretty sharp, I thought. I went up and asked this young lady to dance. She said okay, and we got up and danced. Her name was Lois Jean.

"What are you doing tomorrow night?" I asked her.

"I don't know. You'll have to ask my mom."

"What's your mother's name?"

"Elvira."

I said, "Elvira, can I escort your daughter to a movie tomorrow night? If you give me your address I'll come and get her and take good care of her."

"She's only seventeen, you know. You can't go around drinking and raising cane."

"Oh, no. Nothing like that."

We had quite a few more dates. We didn't talk about getting married or anything. After I got on my next submarine, I wrote letters to her. One time I took a big marker and wrote on a torpedo, "To Tojo, from Lois Jean." Tojo was the Japanese prime minister who ordered the attack on Pearl Harbor. That torpedo hit a Japanese battleship.

After my leave was over, I had a train ticket to New London, Connecticut. That was where the Navy submarine school was. I went to quite a few classes there. Even though I'd been on submarines for seven patrols, these classes were a good refresher for me. This schooling really explained the guts of the torpedo room. I knew how to operate everything in the torpedo room, but I didn't understand all the mechanics of everything until I took these classes. They drummed it all into us. I really enjoyed it, actually. I think a fellow named Joe Bell and I were the only two sailors taking classes there who had already been on war patrols.

From audio recordings made on January 25, 2011, April 22, 2011, and June 12, 2011.

I Was the Old Hand on Submarines

Early in 1944, I watched them send the *Sealion II* down the ways in Groton, Connecticut. This lady, I don't know who she was, hit the ship with a bottle and the boat slid down the ways into the water. Commander Reich was the skipper of the *Sealion*. This lady who christened the boat gave him a cat. So, we had this black cat aboard, named Lucky. We all took care of him. He did okay on the sub. He made it through one war patrol with us. A regular wartime hero. He left the ship at Midway. I think he was adopted by somebody stationed there on Midway.

The *Sealion* was a brand new submarine. There were only eight or ten of us assigned to the boat when it was first launched. They were still working on bringing in a crew for her. We brought the sub up to the dock and started working on it. Every day we went aboard and started learning how to use everything. The people from the shipyard, who built the thing, came out and helped train us. Then we had a few trial runs.

I was one of the senior guys on the crew. I had been on seven war patrols by this time and I was fully qualified to be a torpedoman. Joe Bell was the head guy in the torpedo room. Some guys came on the boat right out of submarine school, but they'd never been on a patrol run. They knew a lot about submarines, but not much about war. Joe and I told them stories about depth charges and what could happen on patrol. These young guys looked up to us. Here I was, not even twenty-one years old, yet, and I was the old hand on submarines.

We left Connecticut and went down to Panama. It was pretty quiet going down the Atlantic coast. The Germans were out there, of course, in German subs. They would have loved to sink us if they could find us. We rode on the surface most of the time, fairly close to the coastline. But not too close; it's a pretty rugged coast and we sure didn't want to run the sub aground. We were out there by ourselves. No

71

escort. All alone. When it was your turn to be on watch with those binoculars, you had to take your job seriously, trying to spot the enemy.

This was my first time going through the Panama Canal. It took us most of a day to get through the locks from the Atlantic side over to the Pacific. We tied up at Panama City. We had liberty all night. Went ashore and visited all the lovely ladies there. We drank a few beers. Everybody in Panama City was making pretty good money off of all the servicemen coming through there.

We went on to Honolulu and did more training with the deck guns before heading out on our first patrol.

From audio recordings made on October 9, 2009 and April 22, 2011.

We Charged in There like a Mad Bull

One time on the *Sealion* we were just south of Korea, riding on the surface in the fog. We had radar and we could see a Japanese freighter standing out just like a sore thumb. It was a pretty good-sized freighter, about 8,000 tons, I think. We went charging in there after him. I was on the wheel. The old man hollered down, "Battle stations! Battle stations surface!" And we all went to battle stations, except me.

I said, "Where's my relief?" My station was in between the tubes, throwing the interlocks, and sometimes I had to fire the torpedoes.

Captain Reich said, "Who's on the helm?"

"Hornkohl."

"Leave him."

That made me feel pretty good. It's a necessary thing to have a good helmsman when you're in a battle. I was so proud that he trusted me. I did everything he told me.

"Left two degrees!" he hollered. I gave it a little twitch, and gave the captain his two degrees. That got him lined up with the target. We charged in there like a mad bull. I'd been through so many battles, I could feel in my gut what was going to happen. We fired three torpedoes from the forward torpedo room. *Uno, dos, tres,* out they went with ten second intervals between them.

I was still hanging onto the helm and we were practically on a collision course. I was thinking, boy, those torpedoes are running hot, straight, and normal. They're going to get there in a matter of seconds. Then the torpedoes slammed into the ship and debris hit the *Sealion.*

So, I was waiting and waiting and the captain didn't say anything. He didn't seem to mind it, but I sure did. I had ahold of the helm and I was ready to give hard right rudder or hard left rudder to get us out of there or we were going to go right through that freighter. Finally, we were down to about 1,200 yards from the freighter; it wouldn't take long

73

to collide with the target from that distance. We came out of a big cloud of fog, and suddenly the freighter loomed up in front of the sub. It had a big hole in the side. If we went into that ship we were going to go down with it. Finally, I heard those beautiful words.

"Hard right rudder!" the captain said. "I mean hard!"

"Hard right rudder! I got it Captain!"

I put my foot in it. The wheel is a big spoke and I had my foot in it to give me some extra umph, and I rode that sucker all the way to the right. I mean I laid into it.

The people that came down afterwards, from the topside, said, "Man, that was a close one." We sank that freighter and we would've gone down with it if we hadn't turned when we did.

From audio recordings made on June 17, 2009 and June 21, 2010.

Pick Up Any Survivors

On our second patrol, we sank two or three ships in a Japanese convoy. Then after all the dirty work was over, we left to go to another place to patrol. About three days later, they pulled the panic button.

"Get back to where you were and pick up any survivors that you can find."

So, we turned around and went back to the area where we sank these ships. Lo and behold, there were a whole bunch of Australians and Englishmen in the water. There had been 1,300 prisoners of war on this big ship that we had sunk a couple days before. We didn't know they were aboard. The Japanese were dingies – they didn't put a red cross on the ship. They didn't notify anybody that they had these prisoners on it. We found out the Japanese ship we sank was the *Rakuyo Maru*.

These guys in the water were just clinging to life. They were all covered with oil. We lowered the bow planes and flooded down into the water so we could grab ahold of them. We brought them up onto the bow planes and then we passed them up to another group standing on deck. We started cleaning them up with mineral oil, which was about all we could use. Anything else would take the skin off them. It was pretty touch and go with these guys. They were in horrible condition. After we got them cleaned, I helped get them down below. I never expected half of them that I took down that hatch to survive.

We brought fifty-four aboard. But, our skipper, Commander Reich, was getting antsy. Because we were sitting out there on the surface picking these guys up, a Jap submarine could come up and nail us. The skipper said, "Clear the bridge. We're diving." Man, we scrambled down that hatch. Really, we practically jumped down that hole. It's just like rats going down a hole. We could have that sub under the water in less than a minute after the dive order. So, we dove and left some guys behind in the water. I tell you, it hurt me very much. I never really understood why we left. I was no authority to say it to the bridge, but we had more room. We had more room.

We found out a lot about these guys once they started to get their strength back. They'd been prisoners three years. They'd been forced to build that railroad in Burma. They called it the Death Railroad. You wouldn't believe how the Japanese tormented and worked them to death. They were malnourished. They had malaria and all kinds of diseases and ailments. When we pulled these guys aboard, they wanted water, water, and more water. We couldn't give them too much water at first. Our corpsman told us what to give them and how to take care of them.

After a couple days, we picked up a doctor from another ship that we went alongside. He was pretty much worthless. Our own corpsman, Doc Williams, knew more than this supposed doctor.

We gave up our beds. We slept on the deck for the next week, getting back to Saipan. We buried four guys at sea on the trip to Saipan. I helped carry the ones who died up through the hatch. They didn't weigh anything, maybe eighty pounds. We didn't even know the names of three of them.

We dropped the survivors off in Saipan. They went aboard the *Fulton*, a sub tender. We shook their hands and waved goodbye. They thanked us for everything. There were tears in everyone's eyes. It was a sad moment, but a gracious one, too. Those guys told us not to blame ourselves for sinking their ship.

Later, Admiral Nimitz had the POWs all lined up and he gave a speech. He said, "We'll get those dirty bastards. You watch. We'll take all of them out. We're gonna do it for you." All the crap they went through at the hands of the Japanese – I could hardly believe man's inhumanity to man.

From audio recordings made on June 16, 2009, February 5, 2010, and April 22, 2011.

It Was the Whole Japanese Fleet

When you were on watch, you rotated through different stations on the ship. You stood an hour on lookout, an hour on the helm, and an hour on the radar. The radar was called PPI. It was a round green circle and it had an arm that swept around. When it hit something, a little pip would show up on the screen. We were patrolling around the Formosa Straits, the straits that go between Formosa and China. It was my turn on the radar and I saw something. I yelled down, "I got something at 44,000 yards!"

"Who's on the radar?"

"Moose."

"Are you sure, Moose?"

"I got him."

So help me God, I picked them up on the radar at 44,000 yards. They didn't believe me. "Nobody can pick up something at 44,000 yards," they said. Then I got a second pip.

"I got two pips!"

"How far?"

"Same. 44,000. Now I got a third one!"

"You got a third one?"

They were beginning to wonder now. So, I said, "Permission to go to my battle station, sir."

"We haven't called battle stations. Stay on the radar."

Finally, I said, "I got six of them on the radar." It was the whole Japanese fleet, what was left of it. These were combat ships, not the old defenseless freighters we sometimes went after. These ships were in a straight line, heading to Japan. We started moving toward the convoy. My relief came and I went to the torpedo room and got in between the tubes.

Joe said, "Are you ready, Moose?"

"I'm ready, Joe." He and I worked well as a team. We could have three tubes ready to fire just like clockwork.

He said, "Make all six ready." They believed me now. They knew we had a convoy in front of us, even though we couldn't see them yet. We were riding on the surface heading toward that convoy as fast as we could. The Japs were moving, fifteen or twenty knots, which is fast for a fleet. We charged across trying to get into position to fire. I had the headphones on. I had to have them on when I stood between the tubes. I had to keep contact with the big guys up in the conning tower.

We got in position. I set the depth at eight feet and we fired the first spread of three off at the first battleship. The torpedoes were running hot, straight, and normal right at this guy. Whammo. Whammo. Whammo. At ten second intervals. We got two hits on the first guy. The second set up was on the second target which was the big battleship. Then we fired the second spread of torpedoes on the second guy. Two of those torpedoes caught a destroyer going across in front of the big battleship. We sank that sucker right there. He didn't stay up for half a minute. Thirty seconds and down he went. He was probably cutting in front to protect the battleship. He sacrificed his crew for the battleship. Then we fired three more from the after tubes.

The big battleship was rolling right along and the convoy was getting away from us. The old man hollered down, "I need those torpedoes ready now!" There were more targets out there and we wanted to get them in the worst way.

I said, "Joe, we only got one choice."

"What do you think, Moose?"

"Well, you're the boss, but if it was me in charge of this room, I'd dump water from the tubes into the bilges." The bilges were these big compartments in the bottom of the submarine, underneath the torpedo rooms. All kinds of water and liquids flowed into the bilges. In order to reload the tubes, you had to empty the water out and get those tubes dry. Normally, we pumped the water back out to sea. But, it was a lot faster to dump all the water out at once into the bilges than to pump each tube individually.

That's what we did. We emptied the tubes into the bilges. We had six tubes, about twenty feet long and twenty-three inches around, so that's a lot of water. We contacted the pump room and told them to turn the bilge pumps on so they could pump the water out. The bilge pumps were going as fast as they could, sucking that water out. We watched the water level gauge on the torpedo tubes and when they got down to empty, we yanked open those inner doors and started loading torpedoes off of the skids.

The skids were along the wall and they cradled the torpedoes. We had to pull the skids into position, lining them up with the tubes so we could shove that torpedo in and get it ready to fire. We put a block and tackle on a ring inside the tube. Then we pulled that block and tackle all the way to the back of the torpedo. Each torpedo had a belly band across it to hold it onto the skid. After we got the block and tackle hooked up, we pulled off the belly band and started pulling to get the torpedo into the tube. You had to pull like the dickens, but you had to be careful, too. That torpedo could come sliding back and land in your lap if you weren't careful. This was going to be tricky because we were rolling up and down on the water. We had rough seas that night.

So me and Bill Lavendar were behind the torpedo getting ready to push. Joe had the rope hooked up to the front.

"You ready, Bill?"

"I'm ready, Moose."

"Okay. Joe, for God's sake, don't slack off on that damn block and tackle; don't let that torpedo come back on us."

"I ain't going to let it come back on you."

I jumped on the skid and put my feet on the propellers of the torpedo and pushed with all my might.

"Bill, push on me!" Bill was behind me with his back pressed up against my back. So, as a team, we pushed and pulled those torpedoes into the tubes. It was a very tricky maneuver. If the torpedo went too fast into the tube, it could ram right through that outer door. We pushed it to the stops. There are stops in the tube that keep the torpedo from going through the outer door. I breathed easy when I heard it hit the stops.

"It's on the stops, Joe."

"I got it from here."

I looked at Joe's line and there was some slack in it. With those loose lines that sucker could have come back on us. If the boat had ridden up on a wave at just the right time, we could have had a three thousand pound torpedo shoved down our throats. We risked our necks getting those torpedoes loaded. We did that six times and got six torpedoes loaded in the tubes. It probably took us about twenty or thirty minutes to get all six loaded.

The sub was going like the dickens. We were trying to catch these guys. The engineers were hollering that we were going to blow the engines. The skipper said, "Keep going!" The engineers always fretted about the engines and the skipper always said crank it up anyway. The convoy was going real fast and the seas were rough. We chased them, but we couldn't keep up with them.

As it turns out, we got the *Kongo*, the biggest battleship in the Japanese fleet, with that first spread of torpedoes. Nailed that sucker right in the middle. But, she ran and she ran. Then she stopped. I heard them say on the headphones, "The target has stopped! She's dead in the water!" Then, all of a sudden, she blew up. It was a tremendous explosion. People said the explosion lit up the night sky making it look like daytime. The Japanese threw down some depth charges, but they weren't even close to where we were. Later, I found out that they thought they were being bombed by airplanes.

If I hadn't noticed that pip, if I'd been asleep, that convoy would have got by us. That night when we sank that big battleship, I felt revenge. I wasn't cheering about the people dying, but the ship was the enemy. That was payback for Pearl.

From audio recordings made on June 17, 2009, October 2, 2010, November 30, 2010, January 6, 2011, and February 17, 2011.

Attacked by a Water Buffalo

After the third run on the *Sealion* we went into Guam. We'd had a pretty tough run. That's when we'd sunk the *Kongo*. We got to Guam and there was a sub tender there and a whole bunch of Marines. So, we pulled in there and our skipper was talking with the Marines and he said, "This crew has been out in the war zone and they're beat."

After being squashed in a submarine for a couple of months and getting chased around by ships and airplanes, your nerves get pretty frayed.

The Marines said, "We'll protect your guys if they want a beer party."

By this time, the Marines had pretty much taken back the island from the Japs. But, there were still a few Japanese loose on the island and they would periodically launch mortars down toward the beach. The Marines were still knocking some Japs out of the caves. Those Japanese wouldn't surrender. They would come down at night and raid the garbage cans. They were starving. I felt a little sorry for them. Nobody should suffer that much. But, they wouldn't quit. So a company of Marines, about 125 guys, set up a perimeter on the beach to protect us. They dug pits and positioned themselves around us. They had machine guns and rocket launchers. They would defend us if the Nippies tried to attack us and bust up our party.

Some places we went didn't have a big supply of beer, like there was in Australia. In places like Guam, beer was usually rationed, two per guy. If you wanted an extra beer, you had to find somebody who didn't drink. They'd save a beer for you. Well, on Guam, the Marines had managed to confiscate a lot of beer from somewhere. They knew where to get the booze. They also had a ton of whiskey. So, we were well-supplied for our beer party.

Our cooks came out from the sub onto the beach and they set up lunch and snacks for the party. Sandwiches and that sort of thing. It was a nice spread. The beer started flowing. We played games, softball, a little touch football. It was just a nice time.

These water buffalo were grazing there by the beach, eating some long grass. I don't know who they belonged to, the natives, I guess. These weren't wild water buffalos. The natives worked them in the fields. I was sitting there with my buddy, Joe Bell.

"Joe," I said, "you've told me how you used to ride bulls back in Texas. See that water buffalo over there? I bet you can't ride that water buffalo."

"Hell, Moose, I've ridden a jillion old bulls before. I can ride a damn water buffalo."

"I don't think you can."

"You guys hold him, so I can get on him."

We started making bets to see if Joe could make eight seconds on the buffalo. We pulled this water buffalo over there, got a rope around his neck, and held him for Joe to hop on.

"I'll show you, Moose. I can ride this thing."

Joe bounced on there just like he owned the world. We let go of the rope, and boy, that water buffalo took out and Joe was hanging on for dear life. That old water buffalo went to bucking. I don't think Joe made the eight seconds. He went flying off and did a couple of somersaults and crash landed on the beach. Joe had a beer in his back pocket. He landed on his butt and broke that beer bottle. He got a pretty serious cut right there on his butt cheek. The corpsman came out and sewed him up right there on the beach.

Joe said to the corpsman, "Doc, does this qualify me for a purple heart?"

"You just bend over there and keep quiet." He sewed him up. We weren't attacked that day by the Japs. We were only attacked by a water buffalo.

From audio recordings made on October 9, 2009 and January 25, 2011.

We Slept Topside on the Hard Deck

After the fourth patrol on the *Sealion*, we pulled into Freemantle, Australia. This was early 1945. I'd finished my eleventh wartime patrol. When we got to Freemantle, I had orders to report back to the States. They needed qualified submariners for new construction. They pulled six or seven guys off of the *Sealion*. We had two weeks leave, though, before we had to head back home. A few of us went up the coast and spent our leave in a nice little town. We had a terrific time. When we got back from our leave, they said, "You're going to the airport. We're going to get you back to the States right away. They really need qualified sub sailors back there."

Altogether, they had rounded up about twenty sub sailors from various ships and they put us on this DC-3 in Perth. That DC-3 was an old two-engine coffee burner; that's what we called it. It was quite a trip getting across Australia to the receiving station in Brisbane. We landed in all these little towns, between Perth and Brisbane. We hopped all the way across Australia. It took us two or three days to get across the country.

When we got to Brisbane, we sat around in that receiving station. The war was grinding down. In that short time from when we first got our orders, things had changed. Getting us back to the States wasn't a big priority anymore. They kept us there for awhile, trying to figure out what to do with us.

One day while I was still at the receiving station, I was in the wash room washing up, getting ready to go to chow. A voice came over the loud speakers. "Now hear this. President Roosevelt is dead."

I didn't see a dry eye in that place. We were really touched bad. These guys were hardened veterans, and here we were walking around with tears rolling down our faces, hugging one another. He was like a father to us. I've heard people say he was a lousy president, but I know he put food

83

in my mouth. I loved him. We finally accepted that we didn't have President Roosevelt as our leader, anymore; we had Harry Truman. Little Harry from Missouri. I don't think there was a finer man in the world than Harry Truman. History maybe tells us a different story, but at the time, I thought he was the tops. He was a veteran in France in the First World War. There was no hiding behind a tree for Harry. He was out there where the action was.

We were still in limbo. We'd been in Brisbane for probably about a month. Then we found out they were putting us on an old troop transport. A great big sucker. There must have been 10,000 troops on there, mainly Army guys, a bunch of Army rangers.

"You sub sailors can handle anything" they told us. "You won't have any trouble on this troop transport."

Being sub sailors, we slept topside on the hard deck rather than go down below. We knew a torpedo could come at us any time. We knew what would happen down below if a torpedo hit that ship. We were rolling through the South Pacific. We weren't going to freeze up on deck.

We even made our own coffee on the deck. All sailors love coffee. We couldn't get anything down below except at meal time. They wouldn't let you come into the galley for a cup of coffee, not like on submarines where you could get coffee all the time. When we could work it, we'd sidle up to one of the cooks and bum a packet of coffee from him. We'd go back on deck with this big old empty coffee can that we had. We'd fill that can with water and put it over a steam valve. There were steam valves all over the place topside. We'd turn the steam on, and, boy, it wouldn't be two minutes and the water would be boiling. Then we'd find the cleanest sock in our gear, put a couple fistfuls of coffee in it, tie it off at the top, and dip it in that steaming water. It made a beautiful pot of coffee.

They had these goofy dudes on the ship. They were pretty wild. These guys had been in Burma, building that long road over there. They'd been in the boonies so long, some of them were nuttier than fruitcakes. We kept the ammo away from these guys.

We went from Brisbane to Auckland, New Zealand. I thought, boy, we're sure to get liberty here. "No," they said. "No liberty for you guys."

Then we pulled into Noumea, New Caledonia. This was a French port at that time. We were pooling our money, getting ready to live it up. They wouldn't let us off the ship. We were all broken-hearted and dejected. Then we stopped at the Fuji Islands. We thought for sure they'd let us out there. They didn't let anybody off the ship. We had one pair of binoculars among us, so we were trading it off. "Let me have a look." We were looking at the beach, trying to get a glimpse of the nice places we couldn't go visit.

We'd been picking up soldiers all along at each stop. I guess they didn't want to turn some of these guys loose, especially those guys who'd been in Burma. So, they just restricted us all. Maybe they were afraid we wouldn't come back. After a stop at Pearl Harbor, we finally ended up in San Pedro, California. We spent thirty-two days out on the rolling seas.

From audio recordings made on July 17, 2009 and June 12, 2011.

We Did More Damage to the Enemy

The war was almost over. I had orders to report to New London, Connecticut again. But, they gave me a thirty-day leave first. I was sitting there at the receiving station in Long Beach, thinking about Lois, the gal I had met in Denver a year and a half before. We wrote quite a few letters back and forth during that time. I called her up on the telephone from Long Beach and said, "Would you like to get married?" She hadn't seen me for a year and a half. It wasn't what you'd call a big, close romance. Evidently, she took a liking to me back when we first met. Maybe it was love at first sight.

"Let me talk to my mom," she said.

"Let me talk to Elvira," I said. I talked to her mom.

"Are you going out on more war patrols?" Elvira asked.

"I'm going back to New London, Connecticut. I don't expect I'll be making any more war patrols. Everything is pretty well done with the war."

I don't know if that made Elvira glad or sad. I'm not sure how she felt about me marrying her daughter. Anyway, Lois and her mother agreed that we could get married. They went to work setting everything up. By the time I got back to Denver, I only had twenty days left on my leave. We rented a hall and hired a preacher. It all jelled up. We got married in June of 1945. We headed to New London. We went on the train, an old coal-burning locomotive with no air conditioning. We stuck our heads out the window to get cool. Our faces were black from coal dust. She'd never been on a train before. I reported in at New London.

"What do you want this time?" they asked.

"I know you got a new sub here. But, I've been thinking about being an instructor on an R boat. Do you have any openings on one of those?"

"We got one for you, the *R-16.*"

The R boats were old submarines that they used for instruction at the sub school. They were training boats. I was in charge of the forward torpedo room. We'd bring students aboard and I helped train them. I hadn't been on that darned boat even a month when we got orders to take her to Philadelphia to decommission it. We rode her down to Philly, to the Navy yard there. Then I went back to the personnel office in New London.

"What else you got for me?"

"We got another R boat for you."

"I hope it ain't going out of commission right away."

"No. This one will be around quite awhile. It's the *R-5*."

I was in New London working on the *R-5* when the war ended. We celebrated downtown. People were screaming and hollering and kissing everybody. That was a hell of a way to finish it, though, with those atomic bombs. I thought about the Japanese and Pearl Harbor and everything that I'd seen. So much loss of life on both sides. What did the Japanese gain by it? It just wasn't worth it in my mind. We lost fifty-two submarines during the war. That's quite a bunch. We were a small segment of the Navy, but we did more damage to the enemy than practically the whole fleet. They didn't pay sailors much then. We did it for our country. We were proud to do it. We weren't out there because we were heroes. We were out there for our country. We were patriotic. Nowadays, pride in our country has been sort of kicked out the window. But, I think these soldiers who've gone to Iraq and Afghanistan are good Americans. We've still got some good ones.

I stayed on the *R-5* up through September and before long, here came the orders to decommission it. I went back to personnel again.

"I don't want any more R boats."

"Don't worry. You're safe. There aren't any left. We're going to put you on the *Cubera*. It's brand new construction."

From audio recordings made on June 17, 2009, October 10, 2009, and June 12, 2011.

PART IV
BETWEEN THE WARS
1945 – 1962

"It was always an adventure. We didn't make a million, but we had fun."

You Have to Go to Sea

I stayed in the Navy on active duty until 1951. I rode three subs during that time. The first one was the *Cubera*. That was a fine submarine. We put it into commission in December of 1945. It was a blistering cold day. There was a blizzard like you've never seen. We had to stand out there on the deck, and my wife was on the docks, too, for the commissioning ceremony. It was a murderous day.

I was the number two man in the after torpedo room. After we did some trial runs, and got everything in good working condition, they told us our home port was going to be Key West, Florida. I thought, that's not too bad. By this time, Lois was pregnant and she wanted to go back to Denver to have the baby. I got her a train ticket and told her that after the baby was born, they could come back down to Key West. She went home, then our daughter Leann was born. I took leave when Leann was born. I had never been around babies. That was really something, snuggling up to our little baby. Things were going great.

In Key West we lived in a little fishing house. It cost forty dollars a month rent. I was a second class torpedoman, and I got a housing allowance, a few extra dollars each month. But, still we could barely get by on my sub pay. The ship's cook on the *Cubera* was an Italian guy named Lopaloosa. He was one fine dude. He knew I was struggling to support my family. On Friday afternoons, he'd say, "Moose, there's a package hidden on the back shelf of the cooler. Grab it when you're ready to go home and stick it under your shirt." It would be some steaks or other food he had left over. He was sticking his neck out a little bit to help me. He wasn't supposed to do that. But, submariners weren't tattletales; if anybody knew about it, they never said anything.

We took the *Cubera* over to Havana and Guantanamo Bay. Cuba was a beautiful place back then. I left the *Cubera* after a year or so and took a 120 day leave. I had

89

built up all this leave during the war. We went back to Denver and I ate up these 120 days and got paid for it. Then, I told Lois I had to make up my mind about the Navy.

"I'm a career guy," I said. "I want to stay in the Navy for my twenty years." She wasn't too happy about that. I was reassigned to the fleet and went to Rhode Island for awhile and worked on torpedoes at the Naval air station there. Then I got assigned to the *Amberjack*. My skipper on the *Amberjack* was Ned Beach; Edward Beach was his proper name. He was quite a writer and a good sailor, too. He wrote books about sub sailors. One was called, *Run Silent, Run Deep*.

Then I got transferred back to new construction, to the *Volador*. We commissioned that sub and did trial runs out of Portsmouth, New Hampshire. We took her down the coast and through the Panama Canal to California. That was my second time through the locks. We operated along the California coast, mainly. Lois and Leann came to California for awhile, but then went back to Denver. I'd have two or three months in port, then we'd be out at sea for a few months. We squeezed in some family life when we could, but when you're in the Navy, you have to go to sea and leave the family behind.

From audio recordings made on June 17, 2009, October 10, 2009, and July 19, 2011.

In the Meantime, I Was Dying

I wanted to stay in the Navy for a career. I didn't want to get out. I had first class in the bag, but I was thinking about leaving. Things weren't going well at home with my wife. The yeoman on the *Volador* was a fellow named O'Neill. We'd been on the *Sealion* together. "Don't sign those papers," O'Neill said. "Don't do it, Moose. You stay in the Navy. Look at all the time you'll be throwing away."

"O'Neill," I said, "I'm trying to hold a family together. I want to do the right thing."

"How do you know you can fix things? You haven't been home in about a year." Which was true. I'd just had a few leaves where I'd run home. God knows how I got to Denver and then back to my assignment on time, riding trains and buses across the country. My marriage was pretty much on the rocks. I didn't know what was going on at home with Lois Jean. I figured that if I wanted to keep the marriage together, I couldn't stay in the Navy.

"Well, you got to make a decision" O'Neill said. "You've got first class in the bag."

"You make it sound awful good. But, I think I'll try to make things work with my marriage." So, I got an honorable discharge and I left the Navy and went back to Denver. This was in 1951.

I went to work at Gates Rubber Company in Denver. I worked the 11:00 p.m. to 7:00 a.m. shift. I worked there a year and never missed a day. I enjoyed my job. I was a tubing operator. I made rubber hose for garden hoses. It was a fast moving job. I had to throw this rubber on this mill and as it rolled through, the friction would heat it up and it would pop and crackle just like a fire. I worked that rubber so it was almost a liquid and then I put it into a machine that pushed it through a die. That's where my helper came in. He would be back there feeding that big strip of rubber into the tuber and it came out as a rubber hose. It came out real fast. I had to throw a big pan, about six feet across, on the table and spin it real fast. Then I'd grab that piece of hose and throw it into the big pan. With my left hand I spun the pan and with my right hand I fed that tube of rubber into the pan so it piled up into a big ring of hose.

It was dangerous work. It was kind of a death trap, really. I had to be awfully careful that I didn't get my arm dragged into those rollers. I didn't dare slack off a bit. We had to produce so many pans of hose per shift. They would give us quotas. Gates Rubber Company was good for putting quotas on us. Every now and then, they'd up the quota and make us turn out an extra pan or two.

One day I went downtown, down to Union Station. I was checking with the railroad just to see what they were doing. Maybe find a job. While I was downtown, I got a big bowl of chili at a diner. I loved chili. I didn't feel good when I got home. But, I had to go to work that night. I just didn't feel good for three or four days. And then I started turning yellow. And I thought, man, this isn't right. We were living with my mother-in-law in her house and Elvira kept saying to me, "Don't go to the doctor. You're all right."

"Did you take a look at my eyes? They're yellow."

"Oh, there's nothing to that."

She was always an optimist. In the meantime, I was dying. I went to work that night. Gates had a nurse on duty all the time, so I went to the nurse there. She sent me straight to the veteran's hospital out at Ft. Logan. As soon as they took a look at me they said, "Man, you've got yellow jaundice. Hepatitis. You're contagious."

"Contagious?"

"Yes, you're contagious."

"So, I can't go back to work?"

"No, you're going to bed."

So, that's what I did. They kept me there about three months. It was beautiful hospital treatment. You couldn't get any better. I was in isolation the first two or three weeks. Then they started bringing in other guys who had hepatitis, too. I think I got it from that chili – from the guy

92

that handled it. They said I didn't just pick this out of the air. I got it from somebody. There was quite a bit of hepatitis going around Denver at that time.

I felt like I was going to die. Miserable. Nausea, weakness, fatigue. I sure was nauseous. I could throw up in a minute. There were two guys in the same ward with me. I told them, "Eat, eat. You got to eat."

"I can't eat. I can't hold it down."

"Man. You better. This is the end of the line. Eat. When they bring that malted milk around, you drink it. Hell, we've all been through more than this."

We were all vets from the war. I just couldn't get to them. They would bring us real rich foods. Malted milk anytime we wanted it. I would drink it. It saved me. It was building my body back up. Both of those guys died right there in our hospital room.

Finally, I went home from the hospital. Of course, I lost my job. Gates was heartless, like most companies. They didn't hold my job open. I didn't have a job, so Lois went to work at a suitcase factory. This is the tragic part, though. I really did everything I could to hold our marriage together. I just wanted things to get better. I knew things were mighty cool between us. One day I was sitting there in the house before she went to work and she said, "I want a divorce."

I kind of gulped three or four times.

"Well, if that's what you want. Any particular reason?"

"No, there's no reason. No use talking."

"Well, we haven't got much. We got the car and we got furniture. What do you want?"

She said, "I'll take the furniture."

"Okay, I can get out of town with the car."

From audio recordings made on March 26, 2009, June 17, 2009, and March 24, 2010.

93

This Will Be a Snap for You

Since I had the car and Lois Jean took the furniture and our daughter, I drove to Toledo, Ohio where my sister Emma and her husband Maurice lived. I worked on the railroad there for a couple months. Then I got word there was going to be a layoff. The railroads were always laying people off. So, I said to myself, "Hell, I've been a sailor and I'm a good deckhand. I'll go down and get my papers for the merchant marines."

I went down and checked into the merchant marines. In order to work on a merchant ship's crew you had to take tests and qualify, that sort of thing. If you passed, you were called an able seaman. There were a few different ratings for able seaman. The higher rate you were, the more money you got. Because of my experience in the Navy, they said I could get my papers to be an able seaman.

"You were in the Navy?"

"Yeah, you bet I was."

"This will be a snap for you. You have to take this test." They gave me an outline of what the test was going to be.

"How soon do I come back for the test?"

"As soon as you think you're ready."

I read all the stuff that they gave me, and after about a week I went back and started the process of getting my able seaman ticket.

"Do you know how to box a compass?" they asked.

"No, but I know compasses. I don't know how to box a compass. I never heard of that." I could follow a course; I was a hell of a helmsman, but I didn't know about this boxing a compass.

"Well, you got to box a compass."

"Let me take this test later."

So I left and went to the library and got a couple of books on seamanship. I went back to my sister's house and my brother-in-law came in there. He was a wonderful guy, a real smart guy. He was a colonel in the Army, but you'd never know it. He didn't lord it over you.

I said to my brother-in-law, "Maurice, I've been in the Navy all these years and I never heard of boxing a compass. I don't know if I can pass this test." Tests always made me squirm anyway. I'm not a good test-taker. I know my limitations.

"Well, I've heard of it," he said. "Let me have that book." He took the book and started looking at it. He was one sharp *hombre*. He went from nothing, a buck private to colonel; he was on the ball.

"Irv, I tell you what. We're going to do this together. But, if I'm going to help you with all this, I want a case of Scotch when you pass this test."

"A case of Scotch? Twelve bottles?"

"Yep. Take it or leave it."

"You're on, Maury."

We studied late into the night for two or three nights. He helped me get it all straight in my mind. I figured out that boxing a compass was memorizing all thirty-two direction points on the compass. Finally, I went down and took the written test. Then they gave me a hands-on test. I had to lower a lifesaving boat into the water. Cast off the lines. Weigh the anchor. Various things like that. I just had to show that I knew my way around a boat.

I passed. I think I had about ninety percent. I qualified at the highest rate for an able seaman, which is right under the third mate. So, I went down to the union hall.

"I want to ship out," I told them. They put my name on the list.

About a week later, they called me and said, "We got a ship for you."

"When do I go out?"

"In two hours." There was no time to fool around. I had to get my gear ready and get down to the docks.

I was assigned to the *John J. Boland*, a ship owned by the American Steamship Company. That was the beginning of my seamanship on the Great Lakes. The *Boland* was an old ship, probably from World War I era. It ran on steam; the boilers were fired by coal. They shoveled that coal in those big furnaces by hand. If you wanted to lose weight, all you needed to do was work in that engine room, shoveling coal all day long.

I was considered a lower officer, so I had my own little stateroom. It was in the forward end of the ship. My quarters were beautiful. The room wasn't big. But, I had a nice desk, a sink, and a good bunk. I didn't have to sleep with anyone else. Nobody in there to dirty up the place. In the Navy, I never dreamed I'd get something like that. The able seamen had their own mess, too.

Because of my experience, I could go up and handle the helm sometimes. That was nice, handling that big old ship. The mate would usually be standing around watching me, but I still had the wheel. Some of those rivers weren't all that wide. There wouldn't always be a lot of room for ships to pass each other. The traffic could be pretty heavy. You had to be real alert with the wheel.

I had my own crew, five men working for me. I was the able seaman of the group. We had about sixteen able seamen on the ship and we were each in charge of a crew of deckhands. We took care of everything on the deck, the winches, the lines, all kinds of gear. We worked around the clock, four hours on and eight off.

We mainly hauled coal, iron ore, and wheat. Most of the time we went into Toledo and picked up coal, from the coal mines around there. This big crane would pick up these coal cars and swing them into the air over the open hold. Then they'd turn the cars over and drop the coal into the hold on the ship. We took the coal to two or three different places. One place was up in Thunder Bay, Canada. After we unloaded the coal, we had to get in the hold and hose it down and make it spotless. We had to have every speck of that coal out of there. I really had to push the crew to do an excellent job of cleaning that hold. We pumped the water and coal dust out into the lake. That's what we did then. Now, they probably don't do that. Some official guys would come aboard and inspect the hold, making sure it was clean enough to load wheat. We put grain in the same hold where we'd had coal. We'd steam down to Duluth where they loaded us with wheat. The wheat came down into the hold in these big chutes. Then we ended up in Buffalo, where we'd unload the grain. We might pick up iron ore or more coal. It took about two weeks to make a round trip. That's what we did for the whole season that I was on the ship. Hauling stuff from one port to another. We went through all the Great Lakes. We would only tie up in port long enough to unload and load back up, usually just about four or five hours.

My crew was pretty stable. Two of them were with me the whole time I was on the ship. They knew their jobs. I kept them in line. Workers are funny. If they find a boss who isn't up to snuff, they'll take advantage.

Most of the deckhands were what we called round-trippers. These were guys that would get on at different ports. They'd stay on for two weeks, a whole round trip. Then they would sign off the ship. They got their pay and would go on a big binge. Spend all their money. Most of them drank up their pay. Then they'd go down to the union halls and wait to hire on again on the next ship. They stayed on the bum until they got back on a ship. These guys would come aboard with no clothes hardly, nothing to their names. Funny what booze does to people. We had a locker that had old clothes in it, jeans and shoes. We'd pass them out to these round-trippers. We'd get them back aboard and after two weeks, they'd look like human beings again, respectable and clean looking. They were good workers, but didn't think beyond their next paycheck.

Some of the people on the ship were career merchant marines. These guys grew up around those lakes. Sometimes, the guys would bring their wives aboard. They might make a trip or two with us.

There weren't that many Navy guys in the merchant marines when I worked on the lakes. I would use Navy language. If we were pulling up the anchor, I'd say "Away

97

anchors, sir! Anchors free, sir!" Instead of what they would say. They might holler, "Hey, the anchor's off the bottom!"

We got into a couple of bad storms that season. Those lakes could get pretty rough, sometimes thirty-foot waves. That big freighter was pretty adept at going through those storms, though. You had to wear a safety belt on the deck during a storm. Guys could get swept off into the water. If the mate saw you without that belt hook on the safety line, you'd get in trouble.

It was a satisfying job. I enjoyed it very much. Not exciting, but the pay was good and the food was good. But, it was pretty isolated. I wasn't isolated on the ship, but I never got ashore. All work, about nine months on the water. At the end of the shipping season, if you stayed on the whole year you got a bonus. For me, that was a good thing. I'd been in that hospital with hepatitis, without work for awhile. I appreciated that money. It was about a third of my pay extra for staying aboard the whole season.

From audio recordings made on June 17, 2009, June 22, 2010, and May 11, 2011.

That Was a Thrilling Date

I met Pauline when I first got to Toledo. My brother-in-law knew her. She worked as a secretary at this place where Maurice did some business for the Army.

"Irvin," Maurice said, "do you want a date?"

"I don't know, Maury." I was kind of reluctant to do anything. I hadn't been divorced all that long.

"There's a nice gal who works as a secretary. Why don't you let me set up a date for you?"

"All right, Maury, I'll take her to dinner."

So he asked Pauline if she wanted to go out with me. Maury fixed the date up for us. I took her out on a cold December night. That '47 Chevy that I had was freezing up on me. I needed to get some water for the radiator, so I pulled up to this exclusive hotel to get some water. I told Pauline to wait for me in the car. I had a little bucket in the back seat and I went into this hotel and found a restroom and filled the bucket. I hauled it back out to the car and put the water in the radiator. Pauline didn't seem to mind, but she must have been thinking I was some kind of bum.

We became good friends but that was about it. I shipped out on the lake freighter pretty soon after we met. If I found out we were going to take a load into Toledo, I'd call her up.

"Pauline."

"Yes."

"It's me, Irvin. I'll be in Toledo in about two hours."

We'd pull into Toledo, and if I didn't have watch duty, I could go ashore for four hours before we shipped out again. We'd go on a date, grab dinner. We had those little dates from time to time. About once a month.

One time when we pulled into Toledo I asked the first mate if I could catch the ship up on the Detroit River. I knew that in Detroit a little boat would pull alongside the ship so we could haul up a mail packet. That little boat would dash out there and match the speed of the ship. We'd drop a line with a hook on it over the side down to the boat.

They'd hook a bag of mail onto it and we'd haul it back up. My plan was to go out in the motor boat and climb up the Jacob's ladder. A Jacob's ladder is a loose, fold up ladder made of rope with little wooden slats for the rungs. Getting on the ship with the mail packet up in Detroit would give Pauline and me a little more time together.

The mate said, "Okay, but don't screw this up and miss the ship."

"I'll be there."

My biggest problem was convincing Pauline that I was going to be all right. "You're going out in a little boat and climb up a rope ladder to get on your ship?"

"That's the plan."

So we drove from Toledo up to Detroit. We went out to the docks and waited for that big ship to come along. When the freighter showed up, I got in that little motor boat and away we went. We pulled up alongside and that Jacob's ladder plopped down there and I had to grab it and jump on. That ladder was swinging around. The ship kept on moving, of course. They wouldn't stop a 10,000 ton ship to load up a delinquent watchman like me. That was a real thrill, believe me. Pauline sat there watching me swinging like an ape on that Jacob's ladder. I managed to climb up without killing myself, which seemed like a miracle at the time. I never did that again. That was a thrilling date.

Things rolled along with the two of us. After the freighting season was over, I checked on the railroad and I couldn't get a job until April. I didn't like the cold weather back in Ohio, anyway. It was monstrous cold in the winter there. I told Pauline I could get a better job working on the railroad back in Denver. We'd talked about getting married. But I wasn't going to commit to anything until I was sure I had a good job. I went back to Denver and got a job with the Union Pacific Railroad working as a brakeman.

From audio recordings made on June 17, 2009 and May 11, 2011.

Sweet-sounding Steam Engines

I loved working on the railroad. The trains had steam engines back then. Diesel engines were starting to come on big, but I worked on the old sweet-sounding steam engines. Those old steam engines were beautiful. The sounds they made were like perfect harmony. Choo. Choo. Choo. Choo.

I got on a good crew. We liked one another and worked well together. We spent about six months hauling sugar beets. During beet season, we worked sixteen hours a day, hauling forty or fifty cars of beets to the processing plant.

I was a brakeman and a switchman. I sat behind the fireman most of the time. When we had to pull off the main track and onto a passing lane, the engineer would slow the train down, pulling up to the switch stand. I'd hop down and run like the dickens to that switching stand. I had a key on a lanyard, and I had to get that key into the lock and pull the lock off and swing that switch handle around. That way the train could switch off the track onto the side and let another train go by. Sometimes while we were chugging along, I'd slip over and sit behind the engineer. I'd say, "Can I get the crossing?" I wanted to blow the whistle at the railroad crossings.

"Yeah, you can whistle the crossing." It's not just little kids who like to hear train whistles.

I did most of my work before we ever left the station yard, moving these boxcars around, getting them hooked up in a long chain. When we'd stop along the way, I had to pull that pin out and kick off cars at different stations. You had to be on your toes, checking the numbers on the cars and making sure you left the right car in the right place.

At times, I was the rear brakeman. I had to ride in the caboose. I was the last person on the train and I had to catch the caboose as the train pulled out of the yard. If I missed that caboose, that was a big no-no. They could fire me. Jumping onto a boxcar, like me and Jack did when we were kids, was a little easier because you could run along-

101

side the train and match your speed. But, with the caboose, you couldn't do that. I had to wait for that caboose to come along. I put my left foot up in the air to hit that step. It was like an acrobatic move to swing up and onto that caboose when it went steaming by. One time the engineer got that train going too fast. I thought, God, I'll never make it. I knew if I fouled this up, I'd be under the wheels. I caught that step and swung up into the caboose. I sure was lucky that time.

Things were working out well. I was making good money and I was with a good crew. I'd been working pretty steady for about six or seven months. The rush was over with beet season and I kept thinking about Pauline back in Ohio. I'd seen her one time since I left Ohio almost a year earlier, but we talked on the phone quite a bit. I didn't have much time for romance when I was working hard and long hours. Before Christmas I called her up and said, "Do you want to get married?" That was the second time I proposed to a woman over the phone. A real romantic.

"Well, yeah, that sounds fine," she said. "Can you come to Ohio so we can get married here?"

The railroad let me have some time off. So back to Toledo I went. We got married in her living room. This was 1953. She moved to Denver and I kept working on the railroad. I worked seven or eight years off and on. I only had a regular crew during beet season. The rest of the time I worked the extra board. That means when they needed an extra person, they'd call you up and say, "Get on down here. We've got a trip for you." I never knew what my schedule would be. I liked it that way. Most people want a regular job, but it takes a long time on the railroad to get a regular, steady job. It was a tough way to make a living, but it was fun, too.

Because I'd get laid off during the slack seasons, I started looking around for other things to occupy my time. That's when I became a prospector.

From audio recordings made on June 17, 2009, June 13, 2011, and August 11, 2011.

We Didn't Worry about Radioactivity

Like other people, I wanted to make a million dollars. The railroad would lay me off from time to time, so I decided to prospect for uranium back in the mountains outside of Hanksville, Utah. Everybody that was anybody was out there looking for a fabulous mine that was going to make them millionaires. There were tons of prospectors roaming around those hills in the 1950s. The government wanted people out there finding uranium. This was the heyday of building big bombs that could wipe out civilization. If you found a good deposit and were able to pull out the uranium ore, the government bought every bit of it.

I had a Jeep pickup with a little six-foot bed on it. My dad and I went to the junkyard and found a wrecked delivery truck. He was good with a cutting torch, so he cut off the back end of that truck. We measured it and cut it just right so it would fit on the bed of my truck. A custom-made topper. I put a brand new Chrysler engine in that Jeep. It was a pretty powerful engine. That truck would practically climb up a tree if I wanted it to. I put two cots in the back, one for Paulie and one for me. We had a little table and a pump Coleman stove, and an ice chest. That's where I would live when I went prospecting. When she could get off from work, Pauline would come, too. We had a lot of fun together, stomping around in the wilderness.

I wasn't a geologist, but I had to study like one. I had to learn what to look for. I studied geological survey maps. I studied up on the likely signs that uranium might be in the area. I'd tromp way back in the middle of nowhere and look for certain formations and features on the landscape. I wanted to find deposits of carnotite, which was yellow. I'd find carnotite on outcroppings of sandstone and on fossilized wood, too. If I found something that looked promising, I'd do a little digging around with a pick and a shovel. A guy who was in the CC camps knew how to use a pick and a shovel. But, with just a pick and shovel, you could be out

103

there forever trying to dig through that sandstone. So, I'd do it the easy way and do a little blasting with dynamite. I'd put about a ten-foot fuse on that stick, light it, and run like hell. I had a little drilling rig, too, that I bought for $250. It had a five horsepower engine. If I found a spot where I wanted to drill, it would take me a few days to set up that rig. I had to position it just right and pour cement to hold it in place. It had a carbide head on it and it would go down pretty deep. It would cut a good hole, right through the rock. I'd pull out some samples and test them with a Geiger Counter. I had a Scintillation Counter, too. It was more sensitive than a Geiger Counter. I would test to see if the sample was radioactive. If you weren't a total dope, you could tell just by looking at your sample if it was good stuff or not. If you found a promising deposit, you might not have hit the jackpot, but you were better off than you were the day before. We didn't worry about radioactivity back then. We were a bunch of dumb clucks out there. That whole country was radioactive; you could hardly miss stumbling onto something radioactive. I'd put a few samples in my pocket and haul it back to the assay office.

Before I went back to town, I had to stake my claim, of course. The claims had to be 1,500 feet by 1,500 feet. I put down rocks in the shape of a T at the four corners of the claim. I had to fill out claim paperwork at the mining office, describing exactly where the claim was. Then I had to file the paperwork at the county courthouse. You had to be awful careful when digging around out there. If you found anything, you had to keep it to yourself, be real secretive until you were ready to sell your claim. Some people would shoot you if you messed with their claim.

I probably filed fifty or so claims over the course of about three or four years. I sold some of them. Most of the people who bought the claims were developers; people with a lot more resources than I had. I got a couple thousand dollars each for the claims I sold, which wasn't bad. But, it was no million.

I met some interesting characters out there. People came from all over. I knew Charles Steen. He was a geologist and he hit it big. He made millions. Charley found a mother lode underground. It was solid Uraninite, the black stuff. Boy, that deposit would knock a Geiger off the chart two miles away. It was a big sucker. He sold his uranium to the government. They just started dumping money in his lap. He built a big mansion in Moab.

One time Paulie and I were out tooling around in the Jeep on a Sunday afternoon. We were going down a back road. Pretty remote, but, still we ran into quite a few people out dinging around. We pulled up to this big wash where the road went down through a big ditch. I stopped at the top and looked around before driving down through there. I could see big clouds and rain in the distance. That rainstorm could be miles away, but the water would come roaring down through that wash, and it could take you right out if you were down in there. This fellow in a car pulled up beside me. He had his wife with him and two little kids.

I said, "Don't go down through there. You might get stuck in that sand and there's going to be a flash flood through here any minute."

He didn't take it too seriously. "I'll just try to get through the ditch and get on my way."

"Have at it, then, buddy."

He drove out there and his car sank down in the sand. That car was stuck. It was just a two wheel drive, a 1950 blue Chevy, a beautiful car. Those wheels were spinning, getting the car deeper and deeper into the sand.

I rushed down there and said, "Give me those kids and get your wife out of there, the water is coming."

He was reluctant. "I don't think there's going to be a flood. It's dry as a bone here."

He wouldn't believe me. I finally convinced him. I grabbed one kid and he grabbed the other and we hauled them up to the top of the ditch. It wasn't five minutes after we all got back to the top, and the water came churning

105

through there. It went right up over the roof of that Chevy. Buried it completely with water.

In the meantime, two or three other people pulled up there. After the water stopped flowing, we went down with shovels and started digging out the car. Two or three of us hooked onto the car with ropes and we pulled at the same time. It was mighty stuck. Finally there was a big sucking sound, and the car popped out of the mud. We pulled it up the bank. That car was a mess like you've never seen. Somebody had to tow him into Moab, and that somebody turned out to be me. I hooked onto that car. Boy, it was just like hauling a boulder. I think the whole engine compartment and every nook and cranny on that car was loaded with about two tons of sand. Pulling that heavy car all that way ruined the engine in my Jeep. When we got to town, I asked him, "Where do you work?"

"I work for Charley Steen."

"Do you work in the mine?"

"Yep, deep in the mine." By this time, Charley had a mine a mile deep that he called *Mi Vida*. They were pulling out tons of uranium.

"I can't thank you enough for what you did," he said.

"Forget that, just get me trip into that mine. I want to see it."

"I can arrange it. I'll clear it with the foreman."

So, Pauline and I went over there the next day and got a personal tour from the foreman. We rode a Jeep deep into that mine.

I eventually gave up the prospecting. The railroad needed me more and more. I started working a regular turn, and didn't get laid off quite as often. We had a good time out there in Utah. It was always an adventure. We didn't make a million, but we had fun.

From audio recordings made on October 11, 2009, October 2, 2010, and August 11, 2011.

Up to My Neck in Snow

One winter I was laid off from the railroad, again. A neighbor of mine said I could get a winter job working for this company out of Oklahoma that installed automatic drillers on big oil rigs.

"I've never even been near a drilling rig," I said.

"Don't worry. I'll teach you everything you need to know."

"All right. I'll take you up on that offer."

The company was Mud Controls Laboratory. I looked into it and they gave me a job working out of Casper, Wyoming. Mud Controls rented out electronic drillers to these oil companies. This equipment that I installed on the rigs would control the pressure on the drill bit. I had to go around to these drilling sites and install them. It took three or four days to get one installed on a rig. I had to weld that sucker on and get all the pieces put together so it would work. Then I had to instruct the people at the rig on how to operate it. Then I had to service it. I'd go around and check it over. Make sure everything was operating properly.

We had these drillers on rigs all over Wyoming and Montana, in all of these remote places. I had a company truck and had to drive all around, dodging moose on those back roads. Pauline would go out on calls with me when she had time. One time we were up near Big Piney, Wyoming. I had installed a driller on a rig up there. This rig was way up in the mountains, above the town. It was snowy and cold. Pauline went up to the rig with me one day. I told her, "Paulie, I don't feel so good. Let's get back down to the motel. You drive."

So we started down the mountain; she was driving down this long, winding road. I started hurting in my stomach. I mean it just kept getting worse and worse.

"Pauline, stop by that snow bank."

"Why, you can't get out right here on this winding road."

"Watch me. Let me out." The pain was excruciating. I got out and I flopped in that snow. Oh, it was cold. You can't imagine how cold it gets up in that part of the country. I needed something to relieve that pain. It was taking me under. We did this two or three times. I'd get back in the truck and she'd drive a ways. Then I'd get out and practically bury my whole front side in that snow. We finally got to Big Piney. The people at the motel called the hospital in Casper and they said they couldn't send a helicopter up to get me because a big snow storm was coming in. They told Pauline it was probably appendicitis and to pack me in ice. We kept that ice machine at the motel running like crazy, keeping ice packed on my stomach. The snow storm hit and nothing could get in or out of that town for about three days. That ice did the trick. I must have frozen my appendix, because by the time we left town, it wasn't hurting anymore. It never did hurt again.

Another time I was up in Big Piney working on this same rig. Pauline was with me again. This darn motel was full. The only thing they had available was a hunter's cabin.

"This is the only thing we got," the guy said.

"Boy, that ain't much. Where's the heater?" The only things in this little cabin were the cook stove and two old Army cots. This was no cuddly bed and breakfast.

"There's no heater, but, there's a cook stove. Just turn the oven on and open the door."

"That's bad news. You can't heat with a stove. That puts out carbon monoxide."

"Well, just open the window."

Man, you could die right away from that carbon monoxide. Paulie and I stayed there and got through it somehow. She said, "Get in this cot with me."

"Neither one of us will get any sleep if we both are on one cot."

"I don't care. Just get over here. It's too cold."

Man, that was a cold night.

Before long, Mud Controls told me they wanted me to go up to Canada, to Calgary, and work out of there. Pauline and I weren't too excited about moving to Canada. I didn't want to be in that cold weather. But, I liked the work and it paid well. So, we packed up and went to Canada. By this time, I had left the railroad for good. They had called me back to work, but I decided to stick with this job. I hated losing my seniority with the railroad. That's just the way it worked out.

I spent a lot of time out in the field in Canada. My daughter Leann was a teenager by this time, and she came up to spend the summers with us. That was real nice. She went out on service calls with me. One time I had to fly in a helicopter up to the Arctic Circle to repair a unit that had quit working. Sometimes, I had to go 600 or 700 miles up north on the ALCAN Highway. I went back into some pretty rough and remote country with these drillers. One place was about ninety miles back off the ALCAN. It was a bearcat to get to. It was kind of dangerous driving on those back roads. There would be big, tall banks of snow along the sides of the road where it had been plowed. There wasn't much room to drive. I'd meet these big trucks going out to the oilfields, loaded with pipe. They'd come barreling up the road, really moving. Whenever I saw that I was going to meet one of these trucks on the road, I drove the pickup as hard as I could into the snow bank. There just wasn't enough room for two vehicles, and that fellow, for sure, wasn't going to put his truck in a snow bank. I drove into the snow bank and hoped there wasn't a big rock buried under the snow. The truck would blast by me and I could hear him hitting the air brakes. He'd finally get that rig stopped about half a mile down the road. Then he'd back up. I was buried up to my neck in snow. I'd throw out a chain, and he'd pull me out. We used the toughest trucks that Ford made. We had to in those brutal conditions.

The weather up there was terribly cold. It didn't make any difference how cold it was; that rig had to run. If there was trouble with the driller, I had to get out there. I was on call all the time, day and night. Even if it was forty-five or fifty degrees below. If I got a call, I had to scramble and get parts and supplies and tromp out into the backwoods to fix that driller. I really had to use my noodle to figure out what was wrong with it.

I was never too happy living in Canada, too darn cold. But, the people were nice and we saw some beautiful country. One time we were over by Lake Louise where they have that beautiful, old hotel. We were out hiking around and we came across this big ravine that the hotel used as a dump. They tossed their garbage and other stuff down in this hole. I looked down there and I saw this old rocking chair.

I told Pauline, "Why, look down there. That's a beautiful old rocker." The hotel staff must have thrown it out. It was probably a pretty early piece of furniture from that hotel.

"Yeah," she said. "I see the rocker. Look over there at those bears." There were a couple bears rummaging through the garbage.

"I see 'em. They're far enough away from the rocker. I think I can get it."

"Be careful."

I slipped over the edge and ran down in that ditch. By this time, some other tourists had come along and were watching me. They were cheering me on. I grabbed ahold of that rocker, and ran back up. I was panting pretty good. The bears didn't even look up. They never slowed down eating.

I hauled that rocker back to Calgary. We had a nice shop at the office where I'd tinker around on things in the evening. I took this rocker all apart. It needed an extensive overhaul. Everything was loose; a couple of pieces were missing. I had a guy with a lathe turn some slats for me. I made a few other pieces. I sanded everything down.

One night I was ready to put it back together. I slathered wood glue all over it, but it wasn't going together like I wanted it to. I made the mistake of trying to put it together all at once. I was getting panicky because the glue was setting up. I let my temper overflow. I picked up the rocker and said, "Oh the hell with it." I threw it down on the floor

110

and smashed it. I went home and I was so sick about what I'd done. I went back the next night and repaired it. Fortunately, none of the pieces had been smashed into splinters. This time I put it together more slowly; I learned from my mistakes. I put a new finish on it and did some hand painting, too, to decorate it. I still have it. It's a beautiful old thing. It has a maple leaf carved in the wood.

We'd been up in Calgary about three years. There was some friction between me and the other guy I worked with. We worked too close together. His wife seemed to think he worked harder than me, and my wife thought I worked harder than him. It was always rubbing someone the wrong way, especially the last year I was there. He came up one day and said, "You're going to have to take this fellow's position up in Dawson Creek."

"I'm not going to Dawson Creek. I've moved as far north as I'm going to. I've frozen my butt off going on service calls up there. I'm not moving there."

So that was it. Time to move on. I wasn't too disappointed about leaving. I'd been working on designing my own driller, anyway. I was setting myself up to be in competition with the same people I worked for. The problem was the oil drilling industry was going into a downturn. I decided to go to Texas. I figured there would be enough drilling going on there that I could sell my driller.

So, we packed up to go from Calgary to Texas. Paulie was working for Williamson Oil and Gas Company. Her boss, Lowell Williamson, was married to Dorothy McGuire, one of the McGuire sisters. She stayed on a couple of months after I left. They hated to lose her. Lowell told me she was the best secretary he ever had.

I planned to drive our VW bug to Texas. I had a guy weld a plate underneath the back end so I could put a trailer hitch on it. I hooked a ten-foot U-Haul trailer up to the VW. I put lots of heavy equipment in there, balancing everything just right.

"You'll never get to Texas pulling that heavy trailer with a little four cylinder VW bug."

"I'll give it a try."

I took out. Everything was going along fine until I got to this long, big hill. It really climbed for quite a ways. With this little VW, if you double-clutched it, you could shift it without grinding the gears. That was my plan. Shift on the fly. I got about halfway up that long hill and I missed a shift and I heard gears grinding. I lost my speed and had to stop in the middle of this hill. There was no way I could start going forward again with all that weight. I had to back all the way down the hill, about a mile and a half. I was real lucky that I didn't meet anybody coming up the hill when I was backing down. That was pretty nerve-wracking. I didn't want that trailer to get sideways and break off and go smashing down that hill. I got it all the way down to the bottom. This time, I put it in low and left it there. Those little four cylinders were just whanging away. I finally got to the top of the hill. Boy, was I relieved. I was lucky all through that deal. That VW made it all the way to Texas with that trailer.

From audio recordings made on July 15, 2009 and August 10, 2011.

PART V
THE SEABEES & VIETNAM
1963 – 1968

*"If someone squealed on me, I
knew I was dead."*

I Wasn't Getting Any Younger

I made a slightly different design on my driller than what Mud Controls was using. I borrowed some ideas from other driller designs, too. I built each unit all by myself. It was a sweet unit. I sold them for $2,500 apiece, installed. I went out and made sales calls all over Texas, driving around and checking out these different rigs. I did a lot of sales work. I sold quite a few of them. But, I just happened to come into it at the wrong time. The bottom dropped out of the drilling industry. I told Pauline, "I've got to do something and bring in more money than I'm making with these drillers."

There was a cotton gin company there in Dallas, where they made these big cotton gins. I applied for a job as a welder. They gave me a bunch of tests, to see if I could weld worth a darn. I did all right and they hired me right on the spot. I worked there for quite awhile.

In 1963, while I was in Dallas, I went to a submarine veterans' reunion. I ran into old Lopaloosa. I had served with him on the *Cubera*.

"How many years did you put in the Navy, Moose?"

"Oh, about eleven."

"That's a lot of time to lose."

"Yeah, I guess it's all over for me and the Navy."

"Why don't you go into the reserves? I bet you can get more time in that way."

I kept thinking about what Lopaloosa said. I had served eleven years. That was a good chunk of my life and I didn't want to lose that time toward retirement. So, I went and talked to the recruiter. At that time, they were actively recruiting people for the Seabees. The Seabees were the construction wing of the Navy. These were the guys who went all over and built bases, and bridges, and roads, and living quarters for the troops. Since I already had eleven years in the Navy, and I had good mechanical experience as a welder and a pipe fitter, they told me I could come back in as a chief petty officer. That was a higher rate than I had when I left. I thought, well, I'm thirty-nine years old and if I don't go back now, I never will. I wasn't getting any younger. So, I joined up on reserve status. The reserve unit in Dallas, though, was full. But, there was an empty billet for a chief petty officer in the reserve company at Corpus Christi, Texas. That's what put Pauline and me on the road to Corpus Christi. We bought a house and four acres of land right on the Laguna Madre for $11,000. The Laguna Madre is a big lagoon between the mainland and Padre Island. Our lots were right on the water. It was nice property, but it kept deteriorating. Water would take the sand out. I built our own seawall. I had tons of rock dumped in there.

I was still selling a few of my drillers, and I got a job back on the railroad again, working for the Southern Pacific. Back to that old routine. Pauline was a stenographer and a top notch secretary. She could handle all kinds of stuff. She had no trouble getting a job in Corpus.

In the reserves, I had to report for drills one weekend a month. We mainly did construction projects. We did a lot of work for the Salvation Army. Renovating old buildings and warehouses. There were about 150 guys in my company, so we could get a lot done in a weekend.

Before long, I had to go to Colorado and get my dad. He was living in a trailer court out in Brighton. By this time, he was in his eighties. The manager there called me up and said, "You're going to have to come get your dad."

"What's the problem?"

"He's had food poisoning. We treated him the best we could. He can't cook for himself anymore; he keeps eating bad food. And, he keeps singing. He sings all day long and people can hear him all over the trailer park."

I packed a bag and took off as quick as I could. I borrowed my father-in-law's big Pontiac and drove straight through to Colorado. When I got there I said to him, "Pop, we're going to hook up your trailer and you're coming back to Texas to live with us."

He wasn't too happy about leaving.

115

"Pop, we got to do it. The trailer park manager wants you to move out, and you can't live by yourself anymore."

So, I hooked up his trailer. We took off and that was quite a trip. As the years had gone by, Pop had started drinking. He was never a drinker when we were growing up. But, by this time, he was hitting the wine pretty hard. I knew he had a stash back there in the trailer somewhere. Whenever I wasn't looking, Pop would slip back into the trailer and get himself a swig or two. Every time we stopped, I'd go back and look for it. Finally, I found the booze and poured it down the sink. He wasn't too happy, at first. But, he got over it. He could accept things like that. He wasn't an alcoholic or anything. It was 1,100 miles back to Corpus, so we talked about old times, and he sang songs. He enjoyed singing. We had a nice trip until I saw a set of flashing lights behind me and I heard this siren wailing. This state trooper pulled me over. He said, "You were speeding." And he told me I had problems with the trailer. The lights weren't right and he listed a few other things he didn't like about our rig. He was ready to write me about five different tickets.

"Why don't you give me a little slack?" I said. "I'm trying to get my father back to Texas. Have a heart."

"Will you promise me you'll stop and get these things fixed?"

I said, "I'll do it." He let me go and I stopped in Wichita Falls and got those things fixed up as quickly as I could.

We got down to Corpus and got Dad all set up. We poured a big concrete pad right beside the house and set his trailer on it. I put up an awning so he had a little covered patio. Whenever I came home from work, we'd sit together on his patio and have a beer. Kind of a father-son thing. That's how we expressed things. How we showed we cared about each other. He never would have said to me, "I love you, son." That would have been impossible for him.

From audio recordings made on June 17, 2009, June 19, 2009, February 18, 2011, and August 5, 2011.

I Had a Stomach Made of Steel

I was in the reserves almost two years. One time, our whole company had to spend three weeks out in California for training. We went out to the Naval Training Center down by San Diego. They loaded us up on a big troop transport and we went out to sea for about two weeks. Every day we went to briefings. They were training us on how to land on a beach. How to hit the ground running and battle the enemy.

One morning they said, "This is it, men. We're going ashore today." We were going to mount an assault on the big beach there at the Navy center on Coronado Island, where the Navy Seals trained. We put on all our gear, full packs, about eighty pounds, and a rifle. As a chief petty officer, I also had to carry a .45 pistol. We were still quite a ways out from the beach. These special landing craft boats pulled up to the big ship. We had to climb down this big net and jump into those boats that were just bobbing up and down on the ocean. They'd load about thirty-five guys onto one boat, then it would back off and another boat would pull up and they loaded that boat. Finally, when everyone was loaded, a flare went off signaling that it was time to head toward the shore. Most of these guys had never been in boats like these. They were flat-bottomed and they rode up and down every single wave. It wasn't a pretty sight. Those guys were seasick, vomiting all over the place. This boat ride was duck soup for me. After all those years on submarines, I had a stomach made of steel.

It took us about an hour to reach the beach. But, we didn't bail out onto the sandy beach. We jumped into water up to our waists. We had to wade through that heavy surf, stepping in darn holes on the ocean bottom. We were pretty well soaked by the time we hit dry land. Then we acted just like we were taking the beach. We simulated blowing up bunkers and charging the enemy in these trenches. Hell, I enjoyed it. It was fun. But, I was thinking the whole time, I sure hope I never have to make a landing like this in a war. To have real bullets whizzing at you when you're out in the open like that would be scary as hell. After it was over, we each had to give a report of how we thought we did.

"How many did you kill?"

"Oh, fifty at least." I think we all hiked up our numbers a bit. We made it through that and I went back to Corpus. Then I got word that I'd been called up to active duty. The war in Vietnam was getting pretty hot, and I knew I was going to be sent back to war. The reserves commander gave me a recommendation and helped with the paperwork so I could go back to active duty as full-fledged Navy, not reserves. I never liked having USNR tagged onto my name. I was always USN. That was so important to me to go back as regular Navy. I told myself, the Navy won't get rid of me before retirement unless they shoot me.

I told Paulie, "Don't you worry, kid. When I get back in there, I'm going to bust butt and be the best chief they've ever seen. We'll get into the regular Navy and we'll go to my assignments together after I get back from Vietnam." She was game. She was no shrinking violet.

Before I left, though, I had to tend to my dad. He couldn't stay by himself anymore, and Pauline couldn't take care of him all the time. We found him a real nice rest home there in Corpus Christi. It was expensive. He had his pension from the railroad, but I had to put up extra money every month to pay for it. He didn't seem to mind going there to live. It was okay with him. Just before I deployed to Vietnam, my sister came and got him and took him back to Colorado. He had fallen and broken his hip and was pretty well bedridden.

From audio recordings made on June 17, 2009 and July 29, 2011.

This Is Right Down My Alley

I reported for duty at Coronado, California. Back to Coronado where we took the beach a couple of months before. Then I went to Davisville, Rhode Island to wait for further assignment. They said to me, "We've got your assignment all lined up now."

"What's the assignment?"

"We can't tell you."

"All right. I'll just wait."

Then they finally called me and two other chiefs into the personnel office and said, "This is hush, hush. Don't tell anyone."

"Okay. What's the plan?"

"You fellows are taking fifty men and you're going to Gulfport, Mississippi to this old Seabee base. You've got to get this base ready because we're going to put a whole battalion down there. Six hundred men. We're going to use this base as a training area before we ship guys off to Vietnam. We want you to clean up the barracks, get the galley ready, and haul off all the crap that's lying around there."

This base had been closed for twenty years. It had been an active Seabee base during World War II, but they closed it down when the war ended. Everything there now was atrocious, bad. There were a few Navy people around there because the base was being used as a storage unit, primarily. But, no troops had been there for years.

It was a big secret because this was all political. It didn't take a rocket scientist to figure out what was going on. There was a senator down there, the richest man in Mississippi, I heard. He and his cronies knew we were going to Gulfport to open up that base. They wanted to keep everything quiet and reap up the goodies. They were positioning themselves regarding the real estate down there, buying property around the Gulfport area because they knew the Navy was going to open this big base. This was going to have a big impact on that little town. We want to have faith in our senators, but they're a little crooked. This is how the government works.

So, there were three chiefs put in charge of these fifty men. One was a machinist. He wasn't too efficient, but he did his job. I got along with him okay. He was out of the reserves. We had another chief; he was a personnel guy. He did all the paperwork. Mantlow was his name. And, then there was me.

They handed me the orders of these fifty guys and we gathered them up and told them to get on down to Mississippi. When I got down there, I looked the place over. It was really a mess. You could hardly live in those quarters. Everything needed an overhaul to make it livable.

Before long, this machinist chief suddenly decided he didn't want to go to Vietnam. He left and went back to his reserve unit. We never saw him again. That left me in charge of everyone. I had to handle all of the physical clean up of the base and get everything functioning. I told Mantlow, "This is right down my alley. You take care of the book work and I'll take care of these guys and get this base running."

I took these guys out for marches and runs. Drilled some discipline into them and then divided them up into working parties. We'd pick a barracks and clean it from top to bottom. It wasn't an easy job. We cleaned up the lavatories, reworked a lot of the plumbing and the wiring. We opened the galley and got it going so we could cook in it again.

I had a brand new Ford pickup. It was a good thing I did, because there weren't any Navy vehicles that we could use. We were on our own. There was a captain who was stationed on another part of the base and I went over there and asked about getting some trucks out of a motor pool.

"We don't have a motor pool here," he said. "You'll have to use your own pickup. Basically, you're getting hosed as far as transportation. Why don't you file some complaints, make some noise about getting some vehicles down here for you to use?"

"I don't want to do that, Captain. I just got back in the Navy. I don't want to make any waves and jeopardize anything."

So, I started hauling all these construction supplies around in my truck. Boy, I tell you, we worked that pickup.

We got everything ready and after about three or four months, the battalion came in. We were commissioned as Mobile Construction Battalion 62, MCB 62 and we got ready to deploy to Vietnam. We had four or five months of training. We did a lot of cross-training for all the different trades. Learning the fundamentals of plumbing and wiring and carpentry, that sort of thing. Then we went over to Camp Lejeune in North Carolina for combat training. We practiced shooting a lot of different weapons and we learned how to operate in a combat situation.

Since I had previous experience with small units, they put me in charge of an advance party of fifty men to go to Vietnam before they shipped the rest of the battalion over. We left in November of 1966.

From audio recordings made on June 16, 2009 and June 23, 2010.

Building a Whole City from Nothing

I was ready to go to Vietnam. It's just something in a military person. Some shy away from it. Some people wonder who in his right mind would want to go to a war zone? I guess some of us military guys have a bit of a fearless attitude. We were trained and we figured we could handle most anything.

I went with this advance party of fifty guys. We flew to Elmendorf, Alaska. We then went to the Philippines. When we landed there, the pilots suddenly decided they needed some rest and recreation. So they announced, "We need two new tires on this airplane."

"We don't have any tires here. We'll have to have them shipped in."

That gave us two or three days to enjoy the scenery. We scattered out. I went to the base and bought a nice camera. They finally put the new tires on the airplane, and then we took off and went to Hue, South Vietnam. Hue was a beautiful old imperial city. There were beautiful temples, monuments, and homes there. From Hue we went down to Phu Bai, to Camp Campbell, our home for the next year. This area was seeing a lot of action at that time. The fighting was right there, all around us.

There was already a detachment of Seabees there from MCB 7. They hadn't built anything to speak of. They built a galley and put it right down in a hole, a galley in the valley, you might say. When the rains came, the water came practically up to your knees in that darn galley when you were trying to get your food. MCB 7 left and we took over.

There was an Air Force helicopter squadron already at this camp and a Marine division with 600 or more guys. The Marines were doing a lot of fighting. This was near the DMZ, the demilitarized zone between North and South Vietnam. The North Vietnamese weren't very far away. There were some Army guys there, too.

122

I was in charge of the advance party. We had to get things ready for the battalion to come. We started working on our own quarters. We built the barracks and we built latrines. Just putting the necessities together, so when the battalion came they'd have a place to live.

When we got our own detachment quarters built, the battalion came and they had a load of supplies. Our job was to take this raw area of ground and turn it into a proper base for the guys out doing the fighting. Like building a whole city from nothing.

The battalion was divided into companies. Alpha Company had road builders and earthmovers. Bravo Company had plumbers and the water people. Charlie Company had builders and construction guys. Delta Company also had builders, carpenters, steelworkers, and roofers. The whole battalion had skilled workers of all kinds. We had steelworkers, heavy equipment operators, surveyors, draftsmen, carpenters, bricklayers, welders, plumbers, electricians; and, we had clerks and bookkeepers and medics and security guys and a chaplain. Everyone had a job.

I was in Bravo Company. I was in charge of everything there at the first with that advance party. Then the officers started coming in and I got pushed back and back until finally I was just a platoon chief. That was okay with me. My platoon had thirty-six men in it.

From an audio recording made on June 23, 2010.

I Did a Lot of Things I Wasn't Supposed To

We got busy and scattered in all directions. We first went to work on the Marine quarters. Getting them a place to sleep; they were sleeping in tents on the ground. We built four and six man hooches. We built these two or three feet off the ground. We put down plywood flooring. Then the sides with studs to hold up the roofs. We put tin roofs on them. They were like cabins. No windows, just bare knuckle quarters. We built them in nice neat rows.

Bravo Company was busy building a water works plant. We dug wells and put in a settling tank. We pumped water into this tank and all the debris settled down to the bottom. The water was pushed through filters, and then it went into great big monstrous tanks. We put in water pipelines all over the place, about 25,000 feet of pipe altogether.

We were doing great and we planned to get water over to the Marines. They didn't have any showers or toilets in buildings. Everything was outdoors. Then the monsoons came and flooded everything. It just poured for days and nights. It rained all the time. Fortunately, we had roofs over most everyone by then.

We had equipment stuck in the mud. Bull dozers sank so deep into the sand and mud, you could hardly see them. We tried to get them out, but they just sank deeper into the sand. It took two or three months to get all our equipment unstuck. We couldn't lay pipe with all the rain and flooding. Some of the pipes that we had laid underground just floated to the surface. We had to use what we called a water buffalo. It was a big tank that held about 500 gallons of water. We hauled that water buffalo up to the Marines so they could get water.

The rain made it steamy. It was humid as all dickens. That rain was hell on morale. The Marines had to go out and fight and patrol around in the rain. My God, when they'd come back, they were battered and torn up. Jungle rot on their feet. All kinds of rashes and infestations. Not to mention a good number of battle wounds and injuries. The hospital was just tents when we first got to camp. They plopped those guys down there in those tents and operated. We eventually built a better hospital for them.

My platoon built a six-acre landing base for the attack helicopters. These helicopters had big Gatling guns on them. Those guns would put down a string of bullets that no person could live through. When those guns spit out ammo, it looked just like fireworks. If you got caught in that gunfire, you were a dead duck. The VC, that's the Viet Cong, hated them.

Anyway, you couldn't land those helicopters in sand. My platoon had to get the ground all prepped and level. Then, we laid out a big plastic membrane. On top of that we put down this matting; each piece was about two feet wide and eight feet long. We locked all of these matting pieces together. We worked around the clock for about a week to get that helicopter pad put together. It was New Year's Eve and my guys were out there working their tails off getting that matting down. They were all wet and tired; they'd been working twelve hours a day. I went into the club and bought four jugs of Jack Daniels. I threw that whiskey in my Jeep and out I went. Each one of my men got a good swig. I wasn't supposed to do that. I did a lot of things I wasn't supposed to.

When the monsoons were over and things dried out, we built indoor showers for the Marines and installed toilets. We built some nice, regular bathrooms for the Marine officers. We put up some galleys for the Marines, too.

We built an ice plant. We built warehouses for storing food and supplies. We had to build a concrete plant, so we could make concrete. The camp didn't really have roads when we got there; it was more like trails. We graded the roads, cut out ditches, and put gravel down when we could get it.

We had to build an interrogation center over in Hue for Arvan to use; that's the Army of the Republic of Vietnam. Bravo Company put in all the plumbing, bathrooms, kitchen, those kinds of things. I didn't like to go in there. The "interrogations" didn't sit well with me.

We had detachments going all over the place doing work. We worked ten or twelve hours every day. We hardly ever got a Sunday off. Morale got real sloppy after four or five months.

From an audio recording made on June 23, 2010.

Just Like a Big Knife

One night at Camp Campbell, I was asleep in my hooch. Sleeping like a baby. There were three other chiefs that shared my hooch with me. About one o'clock in the morning, the VC started firing rockets in on us. They wanted to blow up those attack helicopters that were sitting there. But, their rockets weren't any good and they were falling short of the target. They were falling on us and hitting our barracks.

I ran outside and a rocket came screaming in there and hit the roof on a hooch close to mine. Those tin roofs turned into shrapnel that was just as deadly as the rocket itself. This big piece of the roof went flying by me. If I had moved my head just slightly, I probably would have lost it. Cut right off by this big chunk of the roof. That tin could cut a man to shreds; it was just like a big knife. We pulled injured guys out of the hooches and carted them up to sick bay. Bravo Company got hit pretty hard. Their wounds were bad. I'll forever hear the cries of agony that I heard that night.

The attack went off and on for a couple hours. You could hear and smell those rockets coming in; they were stinky things. If you see a rocket coming in, it's too late. It's going to get you. Two Seabees died that night and a lot more were wounded.

The next morning we started working on repairs. We had to put new roofs on a few hooches. We put tin roofs back on them. I hated to do that, considering how deadly that tin could be. But, plywood would have rotted out there in that damp climate.

Once we got everything cleaned up, life went on. We kept working and building away. We started from nothing, really, and made great progress at this camp.

From an audio recording made on June 23, 2010.

The VC Would Tear Up a Road

Shortly before the battalion's tour was up in Vietnam, they asked me if I wanted to go on a special deployment with a thirteen man team. I said, "Yes, I'll do another tour." They put together our team and sent us back to Gulfport for special training. Mainly, we did a lot of cross-training so each guy could be pretty proficient in all kinds of construction work. They trained us for prisoner of war stuff, too, where they washed us down with cold water, put us under heavy interrogation, tried to crack us up mentally, that kind of thing. They drug us into holes; they literally beat up on us. We had to take it. That was our indoctrination into being a POW. Mr. H was in charge of the team. I don't want to say his name because he's probably still alive. He was a lieutenant JG. I was second in command.

After our training, we went back to South Vietnam in early 1968 to a place near Phan Rang. We were supposed to go further up north with the Green Berets. But, when we got to Saigon, they changed our orders to Phan Rang because the Tet Offensive had started. We took our orders from USAID, the U.S. Agency for International Development. They were a service organization. They helped the Vietnamese with financial aid, food aid, housing, just about anything for the people. They were a people to people organization. So, that's what we did. We helped improve the living conditions of the locals. The USAID people were fair; they didn't mess with us too much.

For a thirteen man team, we did tremendous work. We had a bull dozer, a road grader, two dump trucks, a Jeep. We had two welders, two mechanics, one corpsman, a surveyor, an electrician, a plumber, and heavy equipment operators. Everything was a challenge. The VC would tear up a road or blow up a bridge and we'd go back in there and fix it. We also did a lot of special projects in bunches of little villages. We built a couple of schools. In fact, we built a school in the village where the president of Vietnam had

128

family. His mother was from there. When we finished that school, President Thieu came up there for the school dedication. We did more good for the Vietnamese. I actually enjoyed it.

We had our own compound; it was about half an acre, on the outskirts of Phan Rang, right near the mountains. We had concertina wire all the way around it and a bunker on each corner. We hired Nung guards. They were Chinese. We trusted them. We didn't hire Vietnamese to guard us. Some of the Vietnamese would get sloppy and you couldn't always trust them to be on their posts. The State Department paid for the guards and we chipped in, giving them tips. We had eight or ten Nung guards. They'd rotate on shifts so there were three or four on guard all the time.

We had a team house. We built it ourselves out of plywood that we "borrowed" from the Air Force base that was about thirty miles away. We poured concrete for the foundation. Each man had his own little room in the team house. It wasn't a big room, big enough for a bed and a sea chest where we stored our clothes and gear. We installed two showers and two toilets. There was a little kitchen and a common room where we could sit around, read, drink a beer. We never got drunk and flaked out in our common room. A couple of the guys puffed a little pot. Not in the house, of course.

While we were still building our house, Mr. H came back from a trip to Saigon. He was in Saigon a lot. He had a sweetie down there. He was single, a good looking guy. Big and strong. The Vietnamese women were crazy about him.

"Chief, what are you doing?" Mr. H. said.

"We're building a team house."

"I don't want a team house. I want us to live in tents."

"Mr. H, these guys don't want to live in tents. I'll do what you say, but I already cleared it with USAID and they said it was okay to put a house up on the property."

He quit griping at me about it pretty quick. I don't think he really wanted to sleep in a tent. I expect he was mad about it because he hadn't given the order to build the house. He was in Saigon a lot and I didn't have any way of getting ahold of him to get permission to do something. I'd have been squealing on him if I called down to Mr. Olson, the lieutenant commander and said, "Have you seen Mr. H?" So, it was mum's the word. I just coordinated the jobs myself.

We dug our own well, too. Well, we hired these Vietnamese guys to dig it for us. These guys started digging through the sand. After they got going a ways, they put these concrete rings around the edges. They started out with a ring, about a four foot circle, maybe three feet tall. They put this ring in the hole, then they would dig underneath it and the ring would drop down. Then they would put the next ring on top of that. They'd get down in the hole, digging, and throw the sand up in buckets. I thought to myself, boy, somebody's going to get killed doing this. I told them that we always ringed the edges of the hole with plywood.

"Oh," they said, "we don't need to do that."

"What if it caves in?"

"That will never happen, Chief-san." That's what they called me.

"It's your life, but it will probably be my butt if you guys get killed down there."

When they got down to the water, they dove down through the water with a bucket and brought up more sand. They were hard workers. It was beautiful water. We had it tested and it tested fine. We put up a tower about thirty feet in the air with a big platform on the top. We went over to the Air Force base and asked if we could borrow a crane. They brought over a crane and lifted a water tank up onto the platform. We'd pump the water out of the well up a pipe and into the tank, and that gave us water pressure for showers. We lived pretty well.

From audio recordings made on June 16, 2009, March 24, 2010, and February 18, 2011.

When You're Hungry, Anything Is Fair Game

We had two Vietnamese cooks. We had to fire our first cook. She wouldn't stop feeding us nuoc mam. It's a sauce made from fermented fish. Nuoc mam smells to high heaven. She put it on all our food. It almost drove us out of the house whenever she cooked it. I didn't mind it so bad, but the rest of the crew got awful tired of it. It tasted all right, but the smell wasn't so good. It was pretty potent.

"Chief," they said, "we've got to do something. This cook is killing us."

I told her that she had to quit using the nuoc mam. She didn't get the message. So, we had to let her go. We got another cook and we told her, "No nuoc mam."

She did pretty good. She worked six days a week for us. She cooked all kinds of things and fed us three meals a day. We didn't have a commissary to buy food from. We each got $10 a day for expenses, so we pooled our food money and bought all our food on the open market. We were able to afford choice food if we could find it. But there wasn't much choice food in South Vietnam. The chickens looked like they escaped from Auschwitz.

The Vietnamese would catch these skinny animals, I don't know what they were for sure, but they looked like a bobcat. They would chase down these mangy animals and beat them to death and then eat them. I don't know how they got any meat off of them. But, when you're hungry, anything is fair game. I never dug into one of those.

Every now and then, we'd be invited to dinner with the villagers, to thank us for helping them. You didn't know what you were going to eat, but you'd better eat it. We'd go in there and Mama-san would do the cooking on these little charcoal pots. You didn't know if you were eating a cat or what. We'd sit around and talk using sign language. They knew a little English; I knew a little Vietnamese. We'd talk about the VC.

From audio recordings made on June 16, 2009 and February 17, 2011.

Like Genghis Khan

USAID got a drilling rig and we drilled two wells in the village of Phuoc Lap. This was a Chom village. They were descended from people who had come from India. They were a minority group and the last to get anything in Vietnam. So, we wanted to help them. They'd never had water in this little village before. That's why we drilled these wells for them. After we finished the second well, they were getting water out of it, but we wanted to get it a little deeper. I sent Peterson and Cline out there to work on the well.

One day I went out there to see how things were going with the drilling. They were working away. That cable tool on the drilling rig was really pounding a hole into the earth. All of a sudden the village chief came over to me. He was an older gentleman; well, they all got old pretty early over there, so he probably wasn't all that old. He was nervous, starting to act a little strange. When you're in a war zone like that, you look around and you notice things like this. I could tell something was wrong. He was acting like he might take off running any second. I told Cline and Peterson we'd better shut this operation down for the day.

"What's up, Chief?"

"Just listen to me. I think something's going wrong here. Secure the rig and we'll be back tomorrow."

I told the village chief, *"Mai, mai."* That means tomorrow. He understood. He wanted to tell me to get the hell out of there. We started for the pickup. We were loading up our tools. All of a sudden the VC came over the hill firing like crazy. There were probably forty or fifty of them. They started shooting up the rig. They shot up the tires and put about a thousand holes in the thing. We had no way of fending off a group like that. There were only three of us. We practically fell over ourselves getting into the truck. I saw one of the VC slap something on the rig's engine. And I knew what that was. It was plastique, plastic explosives. Then that engine blew up. We didn't engage them; it would

132

have been suicide to take on a group like that. We flew down the dirt road getting off of that hill. We were hot-footing it out of there. That ended the drilling.

I had that gut feeling that they were going to hit us. The village chief knew the VC were out there, and he was telling me with his eyes, get out of here. The VC weren't after them; they were after us. We never finished the well. You couldn't fix that rig. It needed a new engine, new tires, everything. We didn't have the equipment to pull that big rig out of there. I just left it out there; there was nothing I could do. About a month later the USAID people came over and they said, "We want to know where that rig is."

"What, do you think I stole it?"

I was kidding with them. You're out there in the middle of nowhere and you're supposed to be real serious about a darn piece of iron that the VC blew up. They'd already blown up ten thousand pieces of other stuff.

"Well, we want to see it."

"Why? I put everything in the report."

"We want to see it."

"Okay, how about tomorrow?"

"All right. We'll be here."

They said Air America would fly us up there to look at the rig. Air America was supposedly this neutral, civilian outfit. That was a bunch of hooey. They weren't neutral. Air America was really a CIA outfit and they were fearless fliers. The USAID guy said to me, "By the way, you can't carry a weapon because we're going with this neutral organization."

"Well, then, I ain't going."

"Chief, you got to go and then sign this document or else."

"Or else what? What are you going to do? Out here in the middle of nowhere, the enemy's all around and you're threatening me? I'm going out there armed to the teeth. I don't care what you guys do."

So, they came in there the next morning in their Huey helicopter with a big Air America name on it. Like that's supposed to protect us. The VC had no scruples; they'd shoot you out of the air in a minute, neutral or not. I came out of the team house looking like Genghis Khan. I had an M79 grenade launcher slung over my shoulder, a .45 pistol on my belt, four or five hand grenades, and all the ammo I could strap on. I went out there and said, "Are you all ready?"

That USAID fellow about had a stroke. "You can't go like that!"

"Take your helicopter and leave."

"Oh, get in."

They weren't too happy about me showing up armed. But, I never went anywhere without weapons. So, we flew out to the village. I said, "If you really value your life, don't go running around in this village. The VC are all around there. They practically live there."

"Is it really that bad?"

"What have I been trying to tell you? They almost killed the three of us."

"They won't shoot an Air America helicopter."

"Right, uh huh."

So we landed and the village chief and some of the villagers came running up. "Chief-san, are you going to drill?"

"You can't drill with that." The rig was still there in about a thousand little pieces. I asked them if the VC had been coming around.

"No, no, no VC." But I could tell by looking at the chief's face that the VC were right out there. Being with Air America wasn't much of a shield.

So, I said to the guy, "Now are you satisfied that they shot up everything on that rig?"

"Well, I guess so."

Fortunately, the VC didn't show up that day and we made it back to camp.

From audio recordings made on June 19, 2009 and March 16, 2010.

Boy, It Was Like Miraculous

There were guys who tried to get out of Vietnam. We had a guy on the Seabee team who pleaded that he had a hardship at home and he needed an emergency leave. He left and never came back. He was a corpsman, a medical guy on the team. He was supposed to make calls on these different little villages and treat these Vietnamese kids. We called it medcaps. That was short for Medical Civic Action Program. He left, so I did the medcaps.

Whenever we could finagle it, me and a Vietnamese medical man named Mr. Swee would go out to the villages. Swee wasn't a doctor, but he had some medical training. At least I had faith in him; he could give injections. He also worked as our team's interpreter; he spoke good English.

Me and Mr. Swee would head out early in the morning. The Army would send a Huey helicopter to pick us up. We'd get up in the air real quick because there could be snipers. We took fire every now and then. We'd head out into the mountains. We'd go to these little Montagnard hamlets. All the kids would line up. I would wash them. That was my job, to scrub them up with soap and water. Take a big bucket and wash down their little brown bodies. I just loved them; they were good little kids. A lot of times we'd help the mothers, too, if we could.

Mr. Swee would shoot them with vaccines and antibiotics. They had everything, skin sores, you wouldn't believe it all. They all had something wrong with them. We would treat the obvious cases with penicillin and other antibiotics. We'd go about once every week or so. We'd go to different villages. We'd be surprised when we would go back to a village where we'd been two or three weeks before. Boy, it was like miraculous. That penicillin cured a lot. The kids looked a lot healthier than they did before.

From audio recordings made on June 16, 2009 and June 22, 2010.

You Didn't Steal Anything in Vietnam

We stole a Jeep once. Well, we didn't really steal it. That's what they accused us of doing. You didn't steal anything in Vietnam. You confiscated it. This Army Jeep was sitting there on the road and nobody was using it. I didn't have nothing to do with that Jeep. This is gospel, scout's honor. The guys brought it into camp and I said, "Where'd you get that Jeep?"

"Well, it was given to us."

"Sure. It's snowing in Hawaii now, too."

"Really, Chief, this is ours. It was given to us."

Somebody in the Army had left it sitting around. It was a nice one and we really needed a second Jeep. We had one, but Mr. H always used that for himself. So, we drove this Army Jeep around for a couple of months. Then some guys from Saigon came up to inspect the camp.

Mr. Olson said, "Where'd that Jeep come from, Chief?"

"I don't know, Mr. Olson."

"I don't believe you. If that Jeep isn't gone by the next inspection, you're in trouble."

"It will be gone tomorrow."

I told the fellows, "Get this Jeep the heck out of here or I'm in deep trouble."

They drove it over to the Air Force base and left it over there. It was their problem then.

From audio recordings made on June 16, 2009 and February 17, 2011.

136

Did You Kill Anybody?

We only had one day off. That was Sunday. We'd always have a cookout. We'd have beer, pop, and steaks. Beautiful steaks, we'd cook them on the grill. It was just a nice day off.

We had a gravel pit outside of the Air Force base, about thirty miles out. Hanna, one of our equipment operators, was working over in the gravel pit. One Saturday afternoon Hanna was driving his front end loader, coming home for the weekend from the gravel pit.

Hanna was coming down the road and he got hung up in one of those little beer stands. There were jillions of them along the road. These GIs would come along and get themselves a hot beer. Hanna had quite a few beers under his belt from this beer stand, and he was just scooting along on that big front end loader. Well, he went off the side of the road and he went down a hill and smashed into Mama and Papa-san's house. He took out the whole dang house. Mama and Papa were at the other end of the house and they were thrown out on the ground. They were saved by the grace of Buddha.

Hanna came back into camp, which was about six or eight miles down the road. He came in there and said to me, "Chief, I got into trouble."

"Oh Hanna, what'd you do now?"

"I ran into this house."

"Did you kill anybody?"

"No."

"Good. We'll take care of it."

I took the truck and went out to the Air Force base for some plywood. Every time they saw me coming, they said, "Oh, Christ, here he comes again."

"Well, I'm on the bum again," I said.

"We'll help you. What do you want?"

"I need about twenty-five or thirty sheets of plywood."

I begged, borrowed, and stole and I got a big load of ply-wood on the truck, and a big load of two by fours.

I told the guys on the team, "We're building a house to-morrow."

"What about our steaks?"

"We'll have steaks on Monday. I'll give you Monday off. But we have to do this project tomorrow."

So, on Sunday we got out there and unloaded all of this plywood. Mama-san and Papa-san were standing over there, and all the neighbors were around there watching to see what these Americans were going to do. We had to clear up the debris from the old house, and then we started building that little hooch. It was nice when we finished. It had two good-sized rooms. We put a tin roof on it. We built it on stilts about four feet off the ground, high enough to keep them out of the water and keep the snakes from coming in. Built them a whole new set of steps. We put in two windows with screens on them. We built the whole house in a day.

They were so happy. They weren't going to sue us; they weren't going to go to the command. We were able to keep the whole thing right there. They came up and told me how appreciative they were that we took care of their house. They said they were only out of their bed one night. They had a lot of firewood, too, from the old house. It sure was scattered after Hanna smashed into it. We built them a better house than they'd ever had in their lives. We cooked steaks the next day.

From an audio recording made on June 16, 2009.

The Night the VC Came to Town

In Phan Rang everybody needed sand bags; they were at a premium. Sandbags protected their lives. They put them near their doors so that mortars and rifle fire wouldn't come through. Just like building barricades around their doors and windows. The VC would hit Phan Rang indiscriminately about every two or three weeks. The VC were vicious; they'd lose ten to get one of us. I didn't really understand them. I never got a chance to talk to a VC. The only ones I ever got close to were dead. I don't know what it was about Phan Rang, but the VC loved to waltz through that town.

I didn't steal sandbags; I confiscated them. I went to the Air Force base, talked to my friends, and came away with a bale of sandbags. One night I was delivering sandbags in Phan Rang. I tried to help as many people as I could. I delivered some sandbags to Monsieur Omrow. He was kind of a mayor, a high honcho in Phan Rang. He was also the manager of this hotel. You could sleep there or get a beer or some grub. I went to his house, and his family and some of his older relatives, the grandmas and papa-sans were there, about eighteen or twenty people. They cooked up a big dinner. I was the only American there. It started getting late, so I headed back toward camp and some Arvan fellows stopped me at the edge of town.

"No go. No go, Chief-san."

When they held their rifles up to your chest you better listen to them. They meant to blow your butt off if you went charging through that barricade. So, I went back to Monsieur Omrow's place. That's the night the VC came to town.

The VC started lobbing M60 mortars in on top of the roofs. In Vietnam they had these tile roofs. The mortars were really whamming in on those tile roofs. While the attack was going on, I was with the whole family at Omrow's. Everybody was real quiet, nobody was talking much. Then all of a sudden these rifle butts started hitting the door. Wham, wham, wham. The door was a big, thick sucker made out of heavy teak. It had big iron staves on it. The VC were right out in the street. I thought, well, Irvin, it's your turn. I really felt like this was the night I was going to die. If Omrow opened that door and the VC saw me there, that was the end of me.

The VC were beating the tar out of that door. I could make out what they were talking about. They were talking about me. They knew there was an American in town and they were out to get him. They were asking for the American. Nobody in the house answered them, even though I could tell the people there with me were getting real shook up. I had a .38 pistol with me but that's all. I didn't have my M16 that I usually carried. If the VC had busted through that door and I started firing at them, we all would have been killed and I didn't want that. I would have walked out, hoping they'd drag my butt off and keep me somewhere. There were a couple of people there that spoke English.

I said, "You tell everybody, don't worry. If the VC break in, I'll make a run for the stairs and get up on the roof and try to escape."

That calmed them down a little bit. If an American was caught in there, no telling what the VC would do with them. They whammed on the door for a long time. The VC were really getting mad out there. Hollering and hitting that door with their rifle butts. But, Omrow and his family held good to their word and didn't open the door. The VC finally moved on down the street. Everybody in there breathed a big sigh of relief.

I stayed there all night. I couldn't sleep. I didn't know if they were going to come back. If someone squealed on me, I knew I was dead. Morning finally came and I went back to camp. In the daylight the VC vanished; you'd think they'd never been there. The VC were just like ghosts.

From audio recordings made on June 16, 2009 and March 17, 2010.

I Could Have Won an Academy Award

We did a lot of work for the Montagnards. They were mountain people, little bitty guys. Montagnards were pure natives of Vietnam, some of the original people there. More native than most of the Vietnamese people. The Montagnards were there first, but they got the dirty end of the stick. They weren't treated very well by other Vietnamese.

We worked in five or six different Montagnard villages. They really appreciated what we could do for them. Not like the Vietnamese. The Vietnamese were more like a gimme gang. What can you give me? There are a lot of people like that in America today, scattered over the country, always crying, "What are you going to give me?"

The Montagnards asked for things they couldn't do themselves. I went up to one of their villages one time. I sat down on the ground with the chief and some others. There was an interpreter there and he told me what they wanted done. They needed a culvert put in over a big monstrous ditch. They took me out on a little field trip to see this ditch. There was just a little path going through this ditch. They needed a proper road over it so they could drive through there when they were harvesting their crops. So, we put in a large pipe, covered it with gravel, and smoothed it out with the bulldozer and made a road going over the top. We did a lot of little projects like that for them.

Another time a chief came to me and said, "Come up to my village and clear out the cactus."

Some of those villages were just ringed by these tall, thick stands of cactus. That cactus could be ten or twelve feet tall. The Montagnards wanted to keep the VC from sneaking into their villages through that cactus. The VC were regular engineers. They'd carve a big hole into the cactus and crawl through the hole into the villages and terrorize the people. They hated the Montagnards. The VC were sneaky little devils; they'd steal the villagers' food. Consequently, some of these little Montagnards villagers were practically starving to feed the VC rascals. The VC would go in and threaten them and haul off the young people. They kidnapped them and made them fight for the VC. They were vicious.

I told the chief I'd send a team up to mow down that cactus with the bulldozer. It was a dangerous job. The VC could come in there at any time and shoot your butt off. And, it was a big job. We figured it would take a few days to push all that cactus out of there. I sent Peterson and Cline out to clear this cactus with the bulldozer. They came dragging back to the base that night.

"We're not going out there again, Chief," they said.

"Why not?"

"That dust is terrible. We were practically choking on all that dirt and dust and cactus. Besides, it's just too dangerous. The VC are all around there."

I could see that this was going to be a revolt.

"You're going out there again tomorrow," I said. "I know it's bad. It's miserable work, but you're doing it."

"No, we're not. This is worse than any job we've ever had. If you think so much of the job, you go and do it. See if you like it."

They were pretty adamant about this. I was, too. I thought a minute about how to handle this. I decided that teaching by example would be better than putting the guys on restriction for disobeying an order. I was still pretty mad, though.

"You go out there and wash that damn bulldozer down," I said. "Get it cleaned up and gassed up. I'm taking it out tomorrow and mow down that cactus myself."

"You can't go out there by yourself, Chief."

"Why not?"

"The VC will knock you off in a minute."

"No they won't. Just do what I tell you."

So, they got the equipment all cleaned and ready to go. The next day I went out there by myself. Man, it was hot and humid. That dirt was flying. I think half the dirt in that whole place settled right down on me. I must have had

142

dirt an inch thick all over me. I pushed over cactus and shoved it into big piles until eight o'clock that night. It was rough work. I staggered back into camp, feeling like I was barely alive. But, when I walked into the team house, I could have won an Academy Award for my performance.

"Well, what'd you think of pushing over that cactus?" they asked.

"Hell," I said, "it was a piece of cake. I'm still alive, too, aren't I?" I wouldn't admit to those young guys that I was suffering. And, man, I really was suffering. I walked into my room and collapsed into bed.

Mr. H found out about that incident. God knows where he was at the time. The scuttlebutt just got around. He put that in my fitness report as a criticism. He said that I was leading by example rather than enforcing discipline. He said I let the men get away with too many things.

Anyway, we got the cactus away from this village. The chief came out to me one day and gave me a copper bracelet.

He said to me, "Once you wear this bracelet, you're part of the tribe. You're a Montagnard brother." That made me feel pretty proud.

From audio recordings made on June 16, 2009, June 17, 2009, and February 18, 2011.

Irvin with Vietnamese women, 1968

143

I Went Flying off That Bridge

The VC loved blowing up bridges. They must have sat around their camps and said to each other, "Hey, we don't have anything going on tonight. Let's go out and blow up a couple of bridges."

If the VC came and blew up a bridge or a road, a village chief would come to us and say, "VC come."

And I'd say, "What VC do?"

"Blow up bridge."

"What village?"

He'd tell me which way to get to his village. Then I would take the Jeep and go out and survey the damage. We made a lot of makeshift repairs. We could hardly build anything permanent in Vietnam. The VC would come back and blow it up again. A lot of times we'd build a bridge out of corrugated iron that we could just bolt together. We did that rather than put up a whole structure. That way we could build or repair the bridge quickly. I'd talk to the village chief and say, "I need somebody to put the bolts in the bridge." I'd insist on having the locals help. Sometimes, they'd act like they didn't know what I was talking about, but I'd get to them one way or another. They'd send villagers out to help. Usually, they liked working with us. Anybody from the village could come and help with our projects. Sometimes women would come out and help, breaking rocks, whatever help we needed. We tried to train the locals on how to do these construction projects on their own.

Close to us, only a quarter of a mile or so from our compound, was a pretty substantial bridge. This bridge was on a main road from Saigon that went north all the way to the DMZ. The bridge went across a big ditch; there was muddy, yucky crap down in that ditch. It was about ten or fifteen feet from the bridge down to the bottom of the ditch. Every time the VC came by there, they would kill the Arvan guards who were posted on each end of the bridge. Those Arvan guards had trouble fighting their way out of a wet

144

paper sack. They weren't real fighters; they didn't put their hearts in it. Anyway, when the VC were in the neighborhood, they'd try to blow up this bridge. But, they didn't do too good a job on it. They blew it not long after we got to Vietnam. We got the Air Force to come out with a crane and lift some of the big beams for us and we fixed the bridge.

Then the VC decided to blow it up again. They came up that big ditch one night, killed the guards, and set plastique on the big central iron beams that held the bridge together. Then they blew it. From our compound, we could see and hear that there was some action going on down there at the bridge. So the next day we went and investigated. There was a big chunk out of it. The bridge was barely standing. But, we had to fix it somehow because this was an important road.

So, we went to our old friends at the Air Force base and got a crane. Jackson operated the crane and Gainous and I crawled up on the bridge, what was left of it, anyway. We were trying to pick up some pieces with the crane and move them around and cut away all the damaged beams with a cutting torch. Just cleaning up the debris to see what was left of the bridge.

As it turns out, the VC left enough plastique on that bridge to blow me and Gainous to kingdom come. I think they wired that sucker with secondary charges. There could have been a timed device stuck somewhere, or there might have been more plastique and we hit a fuse with our cutting torch. Whatever it was, I made a cut with the torch and all hell broke loose. There was a big boom and I went flying off of that bridge. I made two loops in the air and landed face down in the muck in that ditch. Part of the concrete structure from the bridge came with me and landed on my legs. Gainous flew through the air, too, but nothing landed on top of him. Gainous got up and ran around looking for me. "Where's the chief?"

Jackson brought the crane around and hooked onto the bridge to keep the rest of it from falling on me. There was a live power line lying there in the mud by me. When the crane would swing over and hit the electrical line, it sent a jolt through me. I was taking 220 volt hits down in that mud.

I was in and out of consciousness. Taking that voltage was the toughest part of it. It felt like it was racking my body. But, on the other hand, I think those 220 volts kept me from going into shock. My mouth and nose were filled with mud and I could barely breathe. Gainous finally found me. He scraped the mud out of my mouth and nose so I could breathe. He started pulling me out from underneath the concrete. I grabbed onto the rear pocket of his pants while he was pulling me up and out of there. I ripped the pocket off his pants, and then his pants tore all the way down to his ankle. Finally, though, I was free.

Someone there said, "Go to the Vietnamese hospital."

I said, "I don't think that's a good idea. We can make it to the Air Force base." That was thirty miles away.

My right arm was all busted to heck. It was basically hanging backwards. Plus, I had shrapnel in my face and head. We both had cuts all over. Gainous had a piece of rebar stuck through his leg, and we were both going into shock. So, we had this bright idea of driving ourselves to the hospital. Gainous and I crawled into the weapons carrier. We were both barely conscious half the time. Gainous drove for a ways, and then he'd pass out in the driver's seat. Deader than a doorknob, unconscious. I'd reach over and try to drive. He'd come to, and we'd trade off driving again.

Somebody had called the Air Force and they sent an ambulance for us. They met us about half way. They loaded us into the ambulance and we left the weapons carrier right there on the road.

"How'd you guys drive that weapons carrier?" they asked.

"I don't know."

They rushed us to the base and into emergency and started working on us. They were good doctors. I remember them running me in for x-rays on a gurney. Skin was

146

basically holding my arm together. They fit all the pieces back together and put a cast on it. They dug the shrapnel out of my face. I had some cracked ribs, too. I couldn't breathe very well there for awhile.

That night, of all things, the base came under attack. The VC were lobbing mortars in there. The doctors came in where I was lying on a bed.

"We got to get you out of here and put you in a bunker."

"Don't touch me." I said. "Leave me alone. If you touch me, I'll kill you." Man, I was hurting all over and I didn't want to move even a muscle because everything hurt like hell. They drug me out of that bed anyway and took me to a darn old dirty bunker. I was in this nice bed and I was thinking I'd rather die in bed than in a dirty bunker. But, that didn't matter to them. Finally, after the attack was over, they hauled me back to my bed. That was the second time that day I escaped death.

I was in the hospital about two days. Then the team came and got me and I went back to camp. We continued working on the bridge, putting it back together. We welded that sucker up and had it operational about two weeks later. We even got a formal letter of thanks from the Vietnamese chief of that district for repairing the bridge.

If it hadn't been for Gainous, I probably wouldn't be here today. He pulled my head out of the mud. I probably would have suffocated if he didn't get to me when he did. He saved my life. If Mr. H. had been on his toes, he should have put in for a Bronze Star for Gainous.

From audio recordings made on June 16, 2009, June 17, 2009, and November 22, 2010.

Like Chickens Out of a Coop

A few weeks after I got out of the hospital, I got eight days of recuperation leave. They sent me to Honolulu. Pauline met me there and we had a nice time. After I got back, I could tell that something had happened while I was gone. The team just wasn't operating right. Attitudes were bad. So, I asked a couple of the guys, "What's going on around here?"

"Oh, you've noticed, have you?"

"Yeah, I've noticed. What's up?"

"You're not going to believe this."

"Try me."

"We had a fight here. Pursifull and Mr. H went at it in the yard."

"You're kidding." I could hardly believe it. But, that's what they told me. Pursifull, one of our team members, was no match for Mr. H. Why, Mr. H could have killed half the crew with his bare hands if he wanted to. He was like Arnold Schwarzenegger, great big muscles. When an officer fights an enlisted man, they can cashier the officer out of the Navy. They're supposed to walk away from confrontations. If I had been there I would have stepped in and stopped it. As far as I know, this incident never got reported. This cloud kind of hung over the team for quite awhile. I couldn't figure out why Mr. H didn't seem to like the team.

Not too long afterward, some officers from MCB 62 came down from Da Nang. Mr. H cornered me, "Chief, you've got to take these guys around to the job sites."

"Why? My right arm's in a cast and a sling. I can hardly drive; I can't shift worth a darn. Why don't you take them?"

"No, you do it." I didn't argue with him. I thought, great, here I'll be driving around Vietnam with a busted arm and all these officers in my Jeep. I sure hoped I didn't wreck the thing. So, three or four officers piled into the Jeep and I told the one sitting next to me that he'd have to shift for me. He did it.

Before long, I was called into Mr. Olson's office in Saigon. He said, "Chief, your tour is about finished. Start closing up your projects and get things secure. We've got an airplane lined up to take you back to the States. Here are the orders for everyone on the team."

"Where's Mr. H? Shouldn't he be here to take the orders?"

"Well ...." He had a faraway look in his eyes. I could tell he wasn't going to tell me. "I know your team's in good hands. You'll get them home. You take their orders."

I really don't know what the story was. Mr. H didn't go home with the rest of the team.

We said our goodbyes to everyone in Vietnam. I was ready to go home, but I was real satisfied with all the good things we did for the people there. The Seabees didn't go rushing out there trying to lay the Viet Cong to rest, but there were many times they tried to lay us to rest. We were happy to get out of Vietnam alive. We finally made it back to Gulfport. Then, we all spread out like chickens out of a coop. The first thing I did was put in for embassy duty.

From audio recordings made on March 25, 2009, June 17, 2009, November 22, 2010, and February 17, 2011.

PART VI
CZECHOSLOVAKIA
& CAMBODIA
1969 – 1973

"We figured we were safe unless a rocket hit us."

The Russians Came into Town

Every American embassy has a resident Seabee, and that is pretty choice duty. You get to wear civilian clothes; don't have to wear a uniform. You get to hobnob with the elite in the Department of Defense and the State Department. You get to go and live in foreign countries. Countries where people weren't trying to kill you every time you turned around. You had to have done two tours in Vietnam before they'd consider you for embassy duty. I was accepted into the program and the Navy sent me to a special school at Fort Belvoir in Virginia. I took a three month course on refrigeration. I learned how to fix any kind of refrigeration unit and air conditioning unit. This was just a way of adding to the maintenance skills that I already had. I had some other training, too. I learned how to armor vehicles, for example. They taught me how to be a Handy Andy.

Meanwhile, I was waiting for my clearance. Embassy duty is a classified assignment, top secret. They went back into my past to find out everything about me. The investigators even went back to Colorado and asked people about me. Despite my derelict childhood, my top secret clearance went through.

At first they wanted to send me to Africa. "Would you like to go to Mozambique?"

"I've never been too crazy about Africa. I'd rather go somewhere else. But, I'll go where I'm asked to go."

Then this assignment came up in Prague, Czechoslovakia. That sounded fine to me. Off I went. This was August of 1969.

The day before I got to Prague, the Russians came into town. They had invaded the country the year before, but there were more troubles. The Czechs were rioting and protesting, and the Russians decided to roll their tanks into Prague right before I got there. Some people from the embassy were waiting for me at the airport when I landed.

151

They hauled me back to town. Russian tanks and checkpoints were everywhere.

As soon as I walked into the embassy I had to go right to work. I had to go up to the attic and start cleaning up the giant mess they'd made in there. They'd been burning documents as fast as they could. They thought the Russians might barge into the embassy and get their hands on all this secret stuff, all of that hot info. So, the Americans were burning documents like nobody's business. They got the attic so damn hot, that they nearly burned the embassy down.

The embassy was an old castle, three stories high, right in the middle of Prague. It had big monstrous beams up in the attic. So, when they were burning documents, they caught all of those big beams on fire. Somehow, they managed to smother the fire. They knew they had a Seabee coming – me. So they left this sooty, smoky mess up in the attic for me to clean up. When I walked in there, some of the beams were still smoking. Welcome to Prague, I thought.

It was quite a job putting that attic back together. Some of those beams were burnt pretty badly. We had to get a team of Seabees in from Frankfurt to help me repair this attic.

When the Russians rolled into Prague, they lost electricity at the embassy for awhile. They realized they had to have electricity to power that document burner. They asked me what I thought.

"Well, let's get an emergency generator and put it right up here in the attic."

I had to look at different kinds of generators and make a decision. So, I picked out the best one for the job and about a month later, here came these delivery guys with this big generator.

They carried that heavy thing up the back flight of stairs all the way to the attic. That back staircase was barely wide enough for them to carry it up. There were six guys carrying it. They had big straps on their shoulders. I thought, boy, if they lose their grip on that sucker it would take out about four or five guys and they'd all crash down that narrow staircase. But, they got the thing up there.

I had to bolt that generator to the floor. That big thing would have jumped all around when it was running if I didn't bolt it down. I had to wire it up and get it connected. I wasn't an electronic genius, but I could handle connecting the power to this generator.

From audio recordings made on June 16, 2009, June 22, 2010, and February 17, 2011.

He Couldn't Hear Crap

There were probably at least 100 people who worked at the embassy. There was a small detachment of Marines, about twelve guys. And, there were quite a few CIA people there, too. There were all of the attachés and regular embassy staff, office workers, and foreign service workers. There were some people there who I never really knew what they did. Most of them lived right there in the embassy. Some lived in town, off the economy, as we used to say. I preferred living in the embassy. There were a bunch of nice little apartments there. My apartment was one big room. It was very adequate for one person. There was a little kitchen. Given my past experiences with quarters, I considered living in this castle pretty lush.

There was something going on in the embassy all the time. People coming and going. We had some VIPs visit us, too. Three American astronauts came once; I got to meet them. Duke Ellington came to the embassy another time.

From day to day, I never knew what I was going to be doing. I just took care of business each day. The secretaries would have jobs lined up for me. One of our secretaries in Prague ended up right here in Colorado years later. Actually, she became the mayor of Colorado Springs, Mary Lou Makepeace. Anyway, I might have some real simple jobs, like going around and replacing blown light bulbs. Or, if there were some workers who came to replace tiles on the roof, or something like that, I'd have to escort them and watch them.

And I had to burn documents just about every day, usually a couple hours worth of burning. Sometimes the Department of Defense people would shred the documents before they handed them off to me. Otherwise, I had to shred them. We had a great big old shredder. These documents would be messages that had come in, I suppose. I never read any of them. They drilled into us that whole "need to know" concept. I knew I didn't need to know anything that was on those secret documents. So, I wasn't ever tempted to read them. Into the fire they went.

I always had to keep my eyes open for anything suspicious. We had an alarm control panel on the third floor that monitored the attic. We had all of these sensors and motion detectors everywhere, so if anyone got into the upper area we'd know they were there. We were concerned about people getting in there and planting bugs. I usually would go up into the attic two or three times a day and make a swing through there, making sure nobody was up there.

One day I went up to the attic and then came back down to the third floor, and there sat this gunnery sergeant who was supposed to be monitoring the control panel. He was a bona fide combat Marine. He'd been too close to a satchel charge in Vietnam. A satchel charge was a bag full of explosives that the VC would throw at us. Anyway, this satchel charge blew out his hearing. He couldn't hear crap. On this particular day, he must have been daydreaming and half asleep. Man, I looked at that control panel and every one of those alarms was going off, making a hell of a racket. All these lights were flashing, too.

"Gunny!" I hollered.

"Yeah, what is it?"

"You got a problem. All your alarms are going off!"

"Oh, hell!" He got pretty excited right away.

"I just checked upstairs. Nobody's up there. But, you've got to turn off those damn alarms."

He went to securing the alarm system. We don't know what set them off. It could have been a heavy wind. I might have set a couple of the alarms off when I was up there. We kind of laughed about it, but it wasn't all that funny, really. Here we had a guy monitoring the alarms who couldn't hear them when they went off. It was something about the pitch of those alarms that he couldn't pick up with his bad hearing. Not the most secure thing.

From an audio recording made on June 22, 2010.

We Caught the Bugs They Left Behind

One of the main jobs for most of the State Department people at the embassy was to keep an eye on the communists. The Russians, the KGB, were camped right across the street from us. Not even fifty feet away was a pack of KGB people watching us. We were always scared of bugs, listening devices. We never caught anyone on the premises planting a bug, but we caught the bugs they left behind. We'd find them in posts. They'd drill holes in posts, stick a bug in there and plug the hole up with sawdust and glue. Whoever did it was pretty slick. We found bugs everywhere. There weren't bushels full of them, but there were plenty.

We always assumed it was locals who planted them. There were lots of locals who came into the embassy. Maids, janitors, and other kinds of workers. If we needed something repaired, like replacing tiles on the roof, then we hired local people to do that work. We had to watch them like a hawk. But, they still managed to plant bugs. I don't think any Americans on the staff planted the bugs. I don't think we had any double agents working there. I would hope not, anyway.

There was this one CIA man who was in charge of looking for bugs and he'd always haul me along whenever he went bug hunting. He had this little machine that was like a portable x-ray machine. I was a little leery about this machine; I figured it was putting out a lot of bad stuff, radiation. It didn't seem to bother him, though. I never operated it myself; I just tagged along.

The ambassador lived in a nice residence about fifteen minutes or so from the embassy. Whenever he'd leave town for a day or two, the CIA guy would come and tell me that we were going to the ambassador's house that night to do a sweep. We'd go through everything in the entire house, top to bottom. We'd scan chairs, tables, inside the cupboards, in the broom closet, under the beds. We x-rayed everything in the ambassador's quarters. One time we were scanning the

156

ambassador's clothes in his bedroom closet and we found a bug in the heel of his shoe. We took the shoe apart and there was the bug right in the heel. Who knows how that got in there?

The main place we were concerned about finding bugs was the plastic conference room in the embassy. On the third floor we had this room that was made out of plastic. It sat inside one of the other big rooms. It was made out of clear plastic; that way there wasn't any place to conceal a bug. People would go in there for their secret conferences. You could say anything in there that you wanted to. We had to go over that sucker with a fine-toothed comb, making sure there weren't any bugs in there.

Any time they had a conference in the plastic room, I had to go up there and sit outside the room. There was this big radio outside the room, and I had to put on headphones and listen to all the frequencies on this radio. It had umpteen thousand frequencies on it. I had to crank around to all of these frequencies. I was listening to see if I could pick up the guys talking in the secret room. If someone had planted a bug in the secret room, or more likely, a bug on one of the people in the room, I tried to find the frequency they were using. I'd be able to hear what the spies who planted the bug were hearing. I'd strain and listen as hard as I could, but I never picked up a voice from inside the embassy. That was a lucky thing.

From an audio recording made on June 22, 2010.

157

This Russian Jeep Came Wheeling Out

Pauline came over to Czechoslovakia after I'd been there five or six months. After she got there, we moved into an apartment on top of an old carriage house on the grounds of the ambassador's residence. That was a sweet little place.

Pauline was there about a year. She didn't have a job while we were there. She would go out and shop every day, practically. She bought tons of stuff, literally. When we finished the assignment in Czechoslovakia, the State Department allowed us to take home 7,100 pounds of items and I think we met the limit. She bought great big old buffets, real heavy things. She bought a brass bed. Lots of other furniture, too. We bought it with the understanding that we'd sell a lot of it when we came back to the States.

She was a real wheeler-dealer. She did a lot of trading. She traded cartons of cigarettes for things she wanted. A carton here, two cartons there. We got our cigarettes from a little commissary there in the embassy. Pauline would load up on these menthol cigarettes. That's what the people over there wanted. Pauline would come home after a day of shopping and I'd say, "How much did you spend today?"

"Three and half cartons."

We bought a VW Fastback in Wiesbaden, and we drove that car all over Europe. We went to France, Belgium, Holland, Germany, Sweden, Norway, Spain, Italy, even over to Casablanca in Africa. We went to other places, too. All in this VW.

One time we were driving down to Bratislava for a softball game. There were about twelve or thirteen guys from the embassy who formed this softball team. We had a couple of Marines and other embassy people. As luck would have it, we were all good softball players. I could hit a pretty good ball. Somebody had set up this game with a Czech team in Bratislava. So, we piled into five or six cars and we drove together. I was driving my VW. We passed through this little town and from out of nowhere, this

Russian Jeep came wheeling out, and, man, he whammed right into the rear end of my car. Boom. I don't know where that Jeep came from.

Everybody stopped and jumped out of their cars. There were four Russian military officers in this Jeep, and we had about twenty Americans in our cars, the guys and some of their wives, too. I thought, oh boy, this is going to be an international incident. I was wondering if maybe we weren't supposed to be in this area. The Russians had restricted some areas where we weren't supposed to go through.

I could tell right away, though, that those Russians wanted to get out of this situation just as bad as I did. We looked at the bumper on my car, and there really wasn't much damage. Not enough to worry about. One of the Russians knew a few English words.

"You okay?" he asked.

"I'm okay."

"Okay," he said. "Goot bye." And he got back in his Jeep and drove off. He was in a hurry. We were all anxious to get out of there.

We made it to the softball game on time. The Czechs didn't know much about how to play. They just wanted to learn. We explained the rules to them. They didn't have much equipment, either. We let them borrow our gloves when we were at bat. We played two or three games that day. We had a good time.

Not too long after Pauline came to Prague, I had a thirty day leave. I said to Pauline, "Let's go see the countryside. Where do you want to go?"

"Well, I always wanted to see Greece."

"That sounds good to me. Let's go."

We loaded up the VW and off we went. We went into Yugoslavia and Greece and Turkey. We went to Istanbul and stayed there a few days. Then on to Ankara. That's when my sister sent me a telegram. I kept in pretty close contact with her, keeping her informed about where I was.

My dad had passed away. He was ninety-four years old. He was ready to go. Dad could hardly hear. He could barely see. He was bedridden. The last time I saw him, he said, "I've had enough. Give me some pills, son. Just finish it for me now."

"I can't do that, Pop."

I called my sister and she said to me, "Don't come home, Irvin. I'll take care of everything." So, I didn't go. I was pretty shaken up. But, he'd lived his time. It was his time to go. He's buried in Boulder. Every time I go through there, I stop at his grave.

From audio recordings made on June 17, 2009, June 23, 2010, and June 13, 2011.

You've Won a Trip to Scotland

Malcolm Toon was the ambassador in Prague. He was a very smart, official man. He was a sharp-looking man with wavy white hair. I got along fine with him. We didn't have a close relationship or anything. But, we'd talk whenever we saw each other at the embassy. He later went to Russia and was the ambassador there. I remember seeing him on television a time or two. He was involved in some high-level negotiations with the Russians.

One time he got sick. I think it was appendicitis. He had to have an operation. The military doctors said that he could fly over to Wiesbaden, where they have the big American military hospital, for the surgery.

Malcolm said, "No, I'm the ambassador to the Czech Republic and I'll have them operate on me here."

So, it fell on the CIA guy to figure out his security while he was in the hospital. The security detail turned out to be him and me. We had to take turns sitting with Malcolm in the hospital. We sat with him twenty-four hours a day, for about a week. I still had to work my regular jobs at the embassy, too, so I wasn't getting hardly any sleep. After a few days, I told this CIA fellow that we needed more people to help out. He twisted a few arms and got a couple more guys to come to the hospital to help.

We were concerned about the ambassador's safety. We didn't want someone to come in there and kidnap him or try to harm him. But, we weren't armed. I wasn't sitting there in the hospital with a weapon. I guess if somebody had come in there with the intent of harming the ambassador, I was supposed to beat him up. Hit him on the head with an IV pole, I guess. Fortunately, nobody bothered him. Doctors and nurses came and went every day with no incidents.

One day I came into the embassy and they said, "Boy, oh boy, Irvin, you won't believe what's happened!"

"Why, what's happened?"

"You've won the contest. You've won a trip to Scotland! You get to go to Scotland with the ambassador and his wife and all of these dignitaries from Pan Am Airlines."

I didn't know anything about a contest. I hadn't heard about this at all. But, if I won it, that sounded fine to me. I was always game for a new adventure. So, the time came to head out to Scotland. We loaded up on this chartered Pan Am flight. Pauline came along with me. There were a whole bunch of people going along on this junket. Then they started talking about golf. All the wonderful golf courses in Scotland.

"Are you a golfer, Chief?"

"No, I never really played golf."

"Oh, you'll get to see some of the finest golf courses in the world."

We got to Scotland and went to our hotel. The next morning the ambassador's assistant came up to me.

"Are you ready, Irvin? We're heading out to the golf course now. Everything is arranged."

"I don't intend to go to the golf course," I said. "Pauline and I have already rented a car and we're going to tour around Scotland."

"You are?" He looked a little surprised and stammered around a little bit. "Well, we'll have to change our plans, make some other arrangements."

Then it suddenly dawned on me. There was no contest. This was all rigged. They wanted me to come along and be the ambassador's caddy. That's why I was there, to carry clubs, haul suitcases, and take care of the grunt work. They had to get somebody else to be his caddy. Pauline and I took off and went on this beautiful trip all around Scotland. We met back up with the ambassador and the whole crowd for the trip home. Nobody seemed to mind that I had gone off on my own. Malcolm was classy. He never said anything to me about not being his caddy. It didn't seem to bother him.

From audio recordings made on June 23, 2010 and July 19, 2011.

Teebe Saved My Neck

I'd been in Prague about two years. I was enjoying my work there. Then the State Department people got ahold of me and said, "We've got a big favor to ask you."

I thought, oh boy. What now?

"There's been an accident at the embassy in Phnom Penh. In Cambodia. The Seabee there is out of commission. He was playing baseball in a lot with some other guys from the embassy and the Khmer Rouge tossed a satchel charge over the fence. It blew up and he was hurt. We had to evacuate him to Guam to patch him up."

I knew all about satchel charges.

"It sounds like that's a pretty nasty place."

They played it straight with me. "Well, yes, the Khmer Rouge have tried to blow up a few embassy cars. And, there are firefights going on in the city every other night. The Seabee wants out before his tour is up."

That made perfect sense to me. Cambodia was basically in the middle of a civil war. It was a complicated place, politically.

"Look," they said, "if you take this assignment in Cambodia, we'll promise you that your next tour can be anywhere you want. We know you'd like to go to Panama. We can arrange that for you."

I thought, boy, that would be nice. I knew they had beautiful quarters down in Panama and that would be good duty. I could have stayed in Prague. I could have told them I wouldn't go to Cambodia. But, I liked the idea of getting to pick my next duty station. The State Department people always treated me good. So, I said yes.

Pauline and I packed up everything and came back to the States. We saw our families and took care of business. Pauline stayed in the States and off I went to Cambodia. This was 1972.

The embassy was right in the middle of Phnom Penh, a pretty dangerous spot. There were probably about eighty people working there. My job was similar to the one I had in Prague. I burned and shredded documents and I took care of maintenance around the compound. We didn't have to worry about bugs there like we did in Prague. Who would be planting bugs in Cambodia? The Khmer Rouge would rather throw a rocket at the embassy instead of fooling around planting bugs.

I lived in a good little house. It was a small two story house, built by the French. The embassy owned this house; it was already furnished. It was about a mile from the embassy. I had a housekeeper named Teebe. She spoke pretty good English. She was just a little mouse. She was a loyal woman. She ran the house, cleaned and cooked for me. Later, when Pauline came over for a few months, Teebe didn't like her being there. Teebe was the head woman in that house and, to her, Pauline was an intruder.

In Phnom Penh, there was always somebody trying to kill you. That's a fact. If they didn't get you out in the open, on the street, they'd try other devious things. I had guards posted outside my house all the time. They were Cambodians, hired by the embassy as guards. These guys were real dumb-dumbs. One day while I was at work, a man came to the door. Teebe answered the door. The guard should have stopped him and not let him knock on the door. This guy said he wanted to come in the house and use the bathroom.

Teebe said, "No, get out." She saw that he was carrying a package. He pleaded with her some more.

Teebe told the guard, "Take this man away from here. He's bad." The guard didn't want to have anything to do with this guy with the package. The guard might have even been in on it. Anyway, Teebe slammed the door and this guy finally gave up and left. She told me about it later. I know that guy had a bomb in his bag. It was probably one that they dropped down in the toilet. They'd been using bombs like that around the city. They wired up the toilet and as soon as it flushed, the bomb would blow up the toilet and you with it. You were a dead duck right in the bathroom. Teebe saved my neck that day.

Teebe was a good woman. Her husband was a high school teacher. After I left Cambodia and Pol Pot took over, he killed anyone who even looked like an intellectual. I heard that they killed Teebe's husband. A lot of my friends were marched out of Phnom Penh and executed in the Killing Fields.

From an audio recording made on June 22, 2010.

We Blew That Sucker to Smithereens

The guy at the embassy who was second in command was named Thomas Enders. He was a fine guy. I got along with him great. I could talk to him real easily. He was a nice, honorable fellow. He was real involved in lots of things going on behind the scenes there in Cambodia. I didn't work with the top guy there at the embassy at all. Hardly ever saw him.

Right after I got to Cambodia, Enders was in a motor-cade leaving the embassy grounds. The embassy was just one big building. The front of it was right on the street, no fence or anything. There were two Cambodian policemen on motorcycles leading the convoy, and then there were two or three other cars in the procession. I think one of the cars was a dummy car, no one in it except the driver. They always dummied things up a little bit, to keep the Khmer Rouge guessing.

Enders was in this 1962 black Bel Air Chevy. It was heavily armored. Anyway, this convoy pulled out onto the street, and across the street from the embassy there sat a cyclo with no one on it. A cyclo is a little peddle taxi; a three-wheeled bicycle with a little open seat behind the driver. A cyclo could hold two, maybe three people. At just the right time, someone pushed this cyclo loaded with a ton of explosives out at the motorcade and they guessed right. That cyclo hit the car Enders was in and blew up. It blew the car up in the air and it flipped over and crashed upside down on the street. The bomb blast blew the two motorcycle cops to oblivion; they were killed. But, the armor on that car Enders was in was so good, the bomb didn't blow it apart. Enders was trapped inside the car for a minute or two, but he got himself loose and he came out of that car smoking and ran across the street back to the embassy. Enders was a big, strong guy. That blast didn't hurt him but it sure tore up that Chevy.

It was my job to get rid of that car. Since it was armored, we didn't want anyone messing with it to see how we had armored it. I brought in a special team of explosive experts from Frankfurt. We hauled that car outside of town to a big empty field. We put plastique charges in certain places on the car so it would pretty well tear up everything that was left of it. We blew it up. That was actually kind of fun. We blew that sucker to smithereens and left it sitting there in the field, what was left of it anyway. As far as I know, that pile of metal is still sitting there in that field.

From audio recordings made on June 23, 2010 and August 10, 2011.

A Phantom Rolls-Royce

Lon Nol was the president of Cambodia. He had seized power not too long before I got there. The Americans were behind the whole thing. Well, I shouldn't say that. But, it was pretty open knowledge that we were backing him. One day at the embassy, they called me into the office and said, "Irvin, do you know how to armor a car?"

"Yeah, I know a little bit about that."

"Good. We want you to go over to the president's compound and armor a car for him. There have been so many threats on his life, and the Khmer Rouge like to attack people in cars."

"Okay. I can build some protection into that car for him."

They set everything up so that I could get into the president's compound and start working on this car. Here's little old me over there trying to armor this car for the president of Cambodia. It was a Phantom Rolls-Royce, a beautiful car. I still had to do my embassy work; but, just about every day for three months, I'd find time to go over to the president's palace and work on the car. There were always a couple guards hovering around me. They watched me like a hawk. I did all of this work outside on the grounds. There was beautiful weather in Cambodia, sunny, although it was pretty hot and sticky. The humidity was terrific.

This was a tough job. They had the materials ready for me. I used thick, heavy plastic. This plastic could take rounds from an AK-47. I shot into a few pieces to see if that AK-47 would penetrate this plastic. It held up real well. I put 1/2 and 3/8 inch thick plastic inside every crevice that I could get to. I had to tear everything out of this beautiful car. I took the doors apart, pulled all the side panels off. I had to cut this plastic to fit inside the door panels, find a way to screw the plastic on, and then I put the door back together. This Rolls had beautiful leather seats. I pulled those out and put sandbags underneath the seats. I also had to seal the windows, so they couldn't be lowered. Then I put bullet proof glass over the existing glass. I put protection in the trunk and in the engine compartment. When I put that car back together, it looked just like it had before. You couldn't tell it was armored. Of course, I added a lot of weight to it. That car was pretty heavy; I'd hate to push it anywhere.

I don't know if Nol ever even rode in that car. He didn't go out of the compound too much. He had a stroke and he was getting a little frail. I saw him shuffling around outside occasionally, going from one building to another. I never met him, of course. I couldn't get within ten yards of him, he was so closely guarded. People were always trying to kill him. A couple times while I was there working in the compound, I saw these single engine airplanes, they were like miniature bombers, flying over and dropping bombs. None of the bombs landed right close to me, but I felt the blast. Man, when I saw those bombers coming, I hit the deck and crawled under the closest thing I could find. Those bombs would drop down and cause some chaos. Then they cleaned up everything and we all went back to work. People tried to drive cars loaded with bombs through the gates a few times, too. They were always trying to do him in.

After I finished the Rolls, I armored a second car, a Chevy. It wasn't nearly as tough a job as the Rolls-Royce, though. I put sandbags all along the bottom. I didn't tear off all the doors like I did on Nol's car. This was just a car for people who weren't high muckety-mucks like Nol, so they didn't get the full treatment.

It was pretty close quarters in that compound. Everyone knew everyone. I got to know some of these government and military people. They spoke English. A lot of them had been to school in France. They trusted me and knew I kept my mouth shut. These pretty little Army ladies would come out to me while I was working and say, "*Monsieur, café?*"

"*Oui, Mademoiselle.*"

They poured out my coffee in these little cups and gave me a roll or pastry, too. One time, they invited me out to this big banquet. A big, fancy party at this French restau-

169

rant. I'm not even sure what this party was for. I didn't ask questions. They invited me, so I went.

They brought out platters of food. Just one thing after another of all this elegantly prepared French food. Then they brought out a bowl of soup and set it down in front of me. I looked down and there was this bird floating in the soup. It must have been squab, a little pigeon. It still had its head. I thought, I can't eat this. But, I didn't dare refuse it. I didn't want to offend anybody. I signaled to the waiter standing over there with a bottle of Johnnie Walker Scotch. He came over and I said, "Pour me a double." I downed that Scotch before I dug into that bird. I didn't eat all of it, but I made a good show of it. If it hadn't been for those two shots of whiskey, I never would have got that sucker down.

Those government people there at the president's palace were good to me. Overall, I enjoyed that project.

From audio recordings made on June 22, 2010 and August 10, 2011.

I Was Jolted by What I Saw

I had a week's leave while in Phnom Penh. I thought to myself, I'd like to go over to Vietnam. I wanted to see the people I had known before and see what was going on there. Even though the war was pretty well over, I was sticking my neck out. It was still a pretty dangerous place. I bummed a ride on a military plane and got to Saigon. Then I bought a plane ticket to Phan Rang. I felt sentimental about that town, for some reason. I found the hotel manager where I'd been the night the VC came and beat on the door. He told me a lot about what was going on. I went out and saw the bridge that I was blown off. It was still in pretty good shape. Then I walked over to where our team house was. I was jolted by what I saw. It was like looking for a ghost. Everything was gone. The quarters were gone. The plumbing was gone. The water tower was gone. They stole everything. Scavenged the whole thing down to bare rock. All that was left was the concrete slab. I asked some people around there, "What happened to the Seabees' house?"

"Seabees left."

"It looks like everything else left, too."

I decided to go up to Da Lat, a mountain town. I'd seen it from the air before, but I hadn't seen it from the ground. There was a bus that went there. Some people told me, "The VC are still along that road up to Da Lat. If you go it's kind of hairy. They sometimes attack the buses."

"I'll take a chance." I made it there all right and I actually had a nice time, seeing the sights and visiting some people I knew who had moved there. That trip was a good experience. I bummed a ride back to Saigon, then another back to Phnom Penh. I was probably the only guy who went to Vietnam on vacation while there was still a war going on. I put my butt on the line, but got away with it.

From audio recordings made on June 23, 2010 and November 30, 2010.

It Was Like Cops and Robbers

The Cambodian Army had these armored personnel carriers. They could take a pretty good bomb blast. They had a bunch of them stored not far from my house in Phnom Penh. One night the Khmer Rouge came into town and broke into this place where these armored vehicles were parked. They stole about twenty of these vehicles and they were scooting out of town as fast as they could go. They came down the road a half a block from my quarters. The Army was chasing these guys and, boy, there was some shooting going on. It was like cops and robbers; they were shooting up the place. I went outside and saw this battle in the streets. I had an AK-47 and a grenade launcher with me. But, I figured this wasn't my fight, so I didn't get into it. It sounded like a whole army going at it in the streets.

Things like that went on all the time in Phnom Penh. You had to keep your guard up. The city was basically under siege. We had a hard time getting food and other supplies. The Khmer Rouge had control of the big river that came up through the city. Supply boats couldn't get through there. The airport was torn up from being shelled all the time; they had to make repairs just about every day. These big American C-130s would fly in and land at the airport whenever they could. They'd land, open the back end, and kick out these pallets of food and supplies for us at the embassy. Then those pilots would gun it and take off again as fast as they could.

Even though this country was in the middle of a civil war, Pauline came over for a couple of months. She wasn't scared of anything. I don't know what it would have taken to scare that woman. One day she was downtown by herself shopping. I was over at the president's compound armoring the car. I could see the Cambodians were running around talking to each other, pretty excited. I knew something was going on. I asked one of the English speaking guys, "What's going on?"

172

"Big rice riot downtown."

I thought, oh God, Paulie's down there wandering around in those shops.

"I got to go." I grabbed my weapon and went downtown. By this time, there weren't any other shoppers around. Everyone had cleared out. Cambodian soldiers were raiding these shops. They hadn't been paid in months. They charged through the market stealing food and shooting some shopkeepers. Everything was a mess around there and these soldiers were still on the rampage, going around from shop to shop. I searched through a dozen different shops, thinking Pauline would be hiding behind a counter or something. Finally, I found Pauline just wandering around in a shop, looking at everything.

"You got to get out of here. There's a riot going on!"

"A riot? I heard some gunfire."

She just didn't grasp the severity of the situation. I grabbed her by the arm. We were able to find a cyclo driver and he took us home. I told Pauline, "Don't you ever do that again."

It was uncertain times in Phnom Penh. It didn't take much to trigger those kinds of riots in the streets. That was quite a town.

From an audio recording made on June 22, 2010.

It Was Chaos on the Streets

At the embassy, I was the head electrician. The wiring in that building was a horrible mess. My God, I took my life into my own hands every time I went into that electrical room. I had to take care of all of the electrical panels and make sure we had power. I had to reach through bundles of wires to get to the breaker switches. If the power went out, which it did fairly often, I had to start everything back up in a certain sequence so the whole system wouldn't blow up. Whoever wired that thing up did a pitiful job. I could have fried myself in a minute fooling with that wiring. We had generators for when the power was out, and those were a bear to get going.

One day, the Khmer Rouge decided to shake things up in Phnom Penh. They started firing these rockets into the city. These were big stovepipe rockets that they got from China. The attack lasted off and on for several hours. They were firing them from over around the airport, which wasn't too far away. They did this to scare the hell out of the people. In the late afternoon, I went on home during a lull in the firing. Then the rockets really started coming in again.

Pauline and I hunkered down waiting it out. The walls in our house were five feet thick. We figured we were safe unless a rocket hit us. They were landing all over the place. There was a Cambodian army colonel who lived with his family across the street from me. Those rockets were coming in and two or three of them made a direct hit on his house. There was a terrific explosion. Blew the house apart basically. They all survived because they had a bomb shelter. Pauline and I didn't have a bomb shelter, so we were like birds on a wire, just hanging out. Then the power went out. I told Pauline, "Man, I've got to get back to work and get those generators going."

So, I hopped on my little motorcycle and took out. At that time I didn't have a car, just this motorcycle. By this time, everybody in town was trying to get out of town. It was

174

chaos on the streets. Everyone had a motorbike or a scooter. You'd be surprised how many people they would cram onto a motorbike. Whole families. These motorbikes were whipping around every which way, and these rockets were whamming in there, right in the middle of the city.

I came up to this big intersection where there's a traffic circle around a big monument, sort of like the Arc de Triomphe in Paris. The rockets were swirling here and there and some were landing right in that area. About the time I entered the traffic circle, there was a big whooom and this rocket landed right in the street and scattered people all over. There was a guy in front of me on his motorbike with his whole family on that bike, his wife and two kids. I thought he was going to zig, but he zagged and cut right in front of me. I hit the brakes and my bike started skidding sideways. I was about to lay it down on the pavement when I hit him from behind. I flew right over the handlebars of my bike and over the top of his family. I hit the ground and skidded along the pavement on my face. Everyone toppled off of that guy's bike, too, but none of them seemed to be hurt. At least they weren't bleeding like me.

I was bleeding all over. My nose was busted up bad; I knew right away that sucker was broken. I pulled myself off the ground and this guy that I hit came running over there. He was angry at me for wrecking his bike. It really wasn't bunged up too bad. The paint was chipped and it had a few dents, but he made a big thing out of it. Here we were in the middle of a rocket attack and this guy wanted to argue with me about his darn motorcycle. A crowd started to gather around us and everyone was pointing at me. I tried talking to this guy, but we couldn't really communicate too well. I was starting to get nervous. Once a crowd like that gets stirred up, they could beat me to death on the spot. I knew I had to get out of there.

Then, just when things were getting hot, this Filipino that I knew came wheeling up there in his Jeep. He was a civilian mechanic who worked at the embassy. He was on

175

his way to the embassy, too. He saw me in the middle of this crowd of Cambodians. He pulled up and got out of his Jeep. He looked at me and saw blood all over me.

"What's going on?" he asked me.

"I got into a wreck with this fellow."

"I've got to get you out of here."

"I'm all for that. This guy wants money for his motorcycle, but I don't have any money on me."

"Don't say anything. Just keep quiet and I'll take care of this."

He talked to this guy with the motorcycle. He could speak the language real well. He convinced this guy to come to the embassy the next morning so I could give him some money. We pushed my bike over to the side of the road and left it there. This mechanic really saved the day for me. I might have been history if he hadn't shown up. We went on to the embassy. He went to work on the generators and I went to the nurse. We had a civilian nurse at the embassy. She cleaned me up and fed me some aspirin. That night, I went back and got my motorcycle. I could hardly believe it was still lying there beside the street; nobody had stolen it. Then, the next day this guy showed up at the embassy and I gave him about $100, right out of my own pocket. That seemed to satisfy him. That was a pretty good pile of money for this fellow.

Meanwhile, I could hardly stand this broken nose. I was in a lot of pain and it was bleeding down my throat. I told the nurse that I had to get this fixed. We made arrangements for Pauline and me to fly to Bangkok, Thailand to the Army hospital there.

We got over there and they took one look at me and said, "We can't do this kind of plastic surgery here. You'll have to go to one of the Thai doctors."

"Is that safe?"

"Oh yeah. This surgeon is good. We've used him before. We'll send an American nurse over there with you to his operating clinic."

"Let's do it then."

176

I went over there and this Thai doctor did all this plastic surgery on my nose and on my face. It was pretty well torn up. He did a good job; he was a good doc. They hauled me back to the Army hospital where I stayed about nine days or so. Pauline came into my hospital room and said, "My God, what did they do to you?"

"I don't like the way you said that." I hadn't looked at myself in the mirror. "Bring me a mirror."

"You don't want to see yourself."

"Is it that bad?"

"Yep, it's that bad."

My whole face was black and blue and everything was swollen up. Pauline could hardly believe it was me. There was an American family at the hospital with a couple of little kids. They came down the hallway and the door to my room was open. These little kids happened to look into my room, and man, those kids started screaming. I must have looked like Frankenstein to them.

From audio recordings made on June 23, 2010, August 10, 2011, and August 23, 2011.

PART VII
JAPAN
& PUERTO RICO
1974 – 1979

"I took care of all the bitching and growling."

I Had Orders for Japan

I'd been in Cambodia for eighteen months. The State Department figured since I hadn't gone crazy, yet, it was time to get me out of there and on to my next assignment. Normally, they took you off of embassy duty after three years. I had more than three years in already in Prague and Phnom Penh. They had promised me another embassy in Panama after I left Cambodia. That was a promise they broke. I could have made a big stink about it and gone to see the officer at the State Department and said, "I want Panama." But I didn't. I went back into the regular Navy rotation and they said to me, "You can either go to Japan or to Kodiak, Alaska." I figured I'd freeze in Alaska, so I picked Japan.

So, when I left Cambodia, I had orders for Japan. In a way I wasn't too happy about going to Japan. I still had some resentment from the war. But, on the other hand, I always wanted to see that country. I wasn't sure how I would handle working with the Japanese. I didn't know if they were going to be resentful toward me. I knew they hated sub sailors. We choked off their supplies and put down a lot of their ships. The war had been over for about thirty years. Long enough time to let the ashes fall through the grate. The Japanese were the enemy during the war. Yet, I never held too much animosity toward individuals. I figured I could handle working with them one on one.

So, when I was getting ready to leave Cambodia, I asked for permission to fly home via Japan. I wanted to look around and see what kind of job it was going to be. Normally, if I was part of the regular fleet, they wouldn't have allowed me to take this side trip. But, I was working for the State Department and they were more flexible with things like that. They agreed to let me go there.

As I was flying into Japan over the water to land, I felt like I'd been there before. Of course, I stood lookout watches on submarines during the war, and a few times we got close

179

enough to see the shore. But, this was my first time to land on Japanese shores. Once I got there, I looked around and decided this was going to be all right. They didn't force me to go there. I could have gotten a transfer to somewhere else. But, I decided I should give it a try.

From audio recordings made on June 23, 2010, June 13, 2011, and August 11, 2011.

I'm Going to Break You

My assignment was in Totsuka, Japan. I was the chief in charge of maintenance at the Totsuka Transmitting Site. This was the Naval radio transmitting site for the entire Pacific Fleet. The base covered about 160 acres. I was in charge of just about everything that needed to be done to maintain the whole base. It was a pretty tough assignment. We had about a hundred Seabees working there.

One of my main jobs was to keep the transmitters cool. If they got too hot, they would blow and then the system would be down. The air conditioning unit was down when I got there. They had already ordered a brand new $50,000 air conditioning unit. I was in charge of all the installation on this unit. That scared the devil out of me because it was such an expensive piece of equipment. It took us about two months to get it on line and running. Then I found ways to make it run better. I kept the doors open to the room, to allow air to circulate through there. Other people told me we needed to keep those doors closed, and I said, "No. That's what blew out the other unit. It got too hot without enough air circulation."

It ran perfectly the whole time I was there. As soon as I left Japan, they blew up that unit. They closed all the doors and it got too hot.

We had a couple civilians that worked on the base. These were State Department workers. We didn't always get along. They wanted to spend money, and I wanted to save money. I cared about expenses and didn't want to spend government money frivolously. We had one guy there, he was a regular Obama, spend, spend, spend. This civilian sure wasn't for saving the government a lot of money. One time he sent special contractors to look over the big transmitting room. They were going to do some upgrades and just general maintenance. It was going to cost a tremendous amount of money. It was in the thousands of dollars.

"No," I said. "I'm not going to okay that."

181

"You better sign it," this civilian guy said.

"Why?"

"Because I said so."

That didn't hold water with me. "I'm not going to do it. That's like throwing money in the trash."

"You're not used to government contracts are you?"

"Well, I've never worked with them before, but I'm sure learning."

It pissed him off. It never did go through. I wouldn't sign it.

We had a great big tower on the base. On that tower was a big disk, a communications disk. Every so often they would paint it. This government worker came around and said, "Chief, we're going to paint that tower."

"Who's going to paint it?"

"Well, civilians, of course."

"What's it going to cost us?" He told me and it was a tremendous figure.

"There's not even a paint chip on that tower. Why do you want to paint it?" I looked at it from a practical sense and this guy looked at it from a money sense. I always suspected that some of those government workers were getting kickbacks somewhere along the line. I never could prove it and I really didn't want to. That would have been pretty ugly.

Most of the Seabees did their jobs well. But, there were about three of them who were complete duds. One was a thief and a liar.

And, there was one dude who gave me no end of trouble. He was getting ready to retire from the Navy. He was a nut. No way around it. He was an alcoholic, too. There were lots of drugs. He may have been high on drugs half the time. He just wasn't Navy material anymore. One of his jobs was to take a tractor out and mow the grass. I finally had to pull him off the tractors. He would take this mowing machine out there, and his machine would mysteriously hit the antenna stakes. He'd tear up the mowing machines. He did that two or three times.

Finally, I told him, "If you break one more machine, I'm going to break you. We're going to court martial you. I'm going to prove that you go out and intentionally wreck your machines to get out of work."

"You wouldn't do that. I've got nineteen years in."

"Yeah, and that's all you're going to get. Once more, and you're gone." I hated to do that, but I had to do something. I even talked it over with the Admiral.

"I've got plenty of proof that he tore up those machines," I told him.

"Chief, you do the best you can with him. You know why you get all these dopes over here?"

"No, I don't."

"What else are we going to do with them?"

"You could start culling them out of the Navy. In my day, they gave out bad conduct discharges. Boot them out."

"I can't do it. We need the men."

"You ain't got a man. You got a machine-killer."

The Admiral was sympathetic, but he wanted to get out of dealing with it. So, I had to put up with that moron until he left Japan.

Pauline went to Japan with me. We lived on the base. There was a duplex there; we had one side and the base commander had the other side. Those were the only living quarters there. All the other guys lived on other bases and had to commute to work.

Pauline worked for an American company. It was a good job. She loved it. She took the train to work every day. That's how she got to know so many of the locals. They rode the train together. She made friends with some college girls that she met on the train. They wanted to practice their English with her. They wanted to know about American cooking. Every now and then, Pauline would invite three or four over to the house for a cooking class. They just loved it. They'd bring their parents along, occasionally. We'd have a regular feast.

Overall, I found that I met a lot of people in Japan that I thought a lot of. We had Japanese drivers, maintenance

183

people, and carpenters who came on the base to work. We got along okay. I was stationed in Japan for four and a half years.

Every now and then I'd get on a train wearing my uniform and see an older Japanese man sitting there looking at me. To say that he was staring daggers at me would be putting it mildly. He was probably wishing I was deader than a doorknob. I guess if somebody had lived through the bombings that they took from us, I can understand why they might hate Americans. But, I won't forget Pearl Harbor, either. What a rotten thing they did, coming in there like that and wreaking the havoc that they did. I won't ever forget it.

From audio recordings made on June 23, 2010, June 13, 2011, and August 11, 2011.

Don't Go Out and Kill Yourself

I'd always wanted to fly. When I was a kid, I used to go and hang out at Stapleton Airport in Denver, whenever I could get a ride out there. My step-mother used to take us out there, too. She loved to see airplanes. We'd sit out there, her and my dad, all of us, and we'd watch the planes come in and land and take off. And I said, "Someday, I'm going to fly one of those."

"Oh, you don't ever want to fly one of them, Irvin," she said.

"No, Mom, I mean it. Someday I want to fly."

I'd hang around the airports. Help with a little clean up work. Washing the planes down. I always had in my mind that I wanted to fly. Well, I got my chance when I was working in Japan. I heard these guys talking one day about going over to Atsugi and flying. I said, "What have you got over in Atsugi?"

"We got a flying club."

"Do you have instructors?"

"Yeah, we got instructors."

Well, I thought, maybe I'll fulfill that dream. So, I went over there and sure enough they had instructors there. Most of them were Navy pilots. Some of those guys were flying jets; they were good pilots. They gave these lessons mainly because they wanted to get a little money out of it. This was a club just for American servicemen, doing this in their spare time. They called it the Aeroclub. They had two 150 Cessnas, a Cessna 172, and they had a Beechcraft, which was a pretty powerful little airplane.

They started me out with an instructor on a 150, that's a small Cessna. The cost of instructions was very reasonable. I had to buy the gas. But, gas was cheap, thirty-three cents a gallon.

I kept plugging away and plugging away at the lessons, pushing to get my license. I had to take lessons on my time off and I had to do it when the instructors were available.

185

In flight school I had to learn to navigate, put the airplane from point A to point B. I had to learn to do instrument flying. That wasn't too easy for me. It wasn't too bad either. It took me about a year to get my license.

At forty hours you could solo, so I soloed right at forty hours. I was out that day with my instructor, a Navy pilot. We were coming in for landings and going out again. He always put me in the pilot's seat, so I was flying the plane. One of my landings was pretty rickety. The instructor said, "Well, if the wheels are still attached, pull up and let's go up and around again."

On the next landing, which was better, he asked, "Do you still want to solo?"

"I really do."

"All right. It's up to you now." And he just got out of the plane. "Take it out and bring it back. Do your thing and I'll watch you."

I wasn't expecting to solo that day. I didn't know if I was ready or not. I was very apprehensive about it. I wasn't feeling like a real dare devil. I wasn't afraid, but I was worried about making a mistake. I started down the runway. I concentrated on the instruments. That took some of the heat off of my stomach. Helped get rid of those butterflies. I did exactly like I was taught. I hauled her back and she eased up off the ground. Away I went.

I made a big circle around the airport. Then I started my approach and asked for permission to land from the tower. I sank the plane in and landed just fine. I made three loops and three landings. I pulled up there and my instructor came out and signed me off.

"You did all right," he said. "Just don't go out and kill yourself."

I got my license. Then I took more lessons on instrument flying so I could learn to land the plane at night, using just the instruments. The instrument instructor was obnoxious and nasty. Any move I made, he would criticize. After working with him all night, I was ready to jump out of the airplane. He was the only one teaching night flying, so I had no choice but to go with him. It was good training, but rough with this nasty dude.

I joined the flying club; then they made me the safety officer. They knew that I was a Seabee and that I could get heavy equipment if we needed to move something or work on something there at the hanger.

I flew all over Japan. Every time I got a chance, I'd be up flying, mainly just day trips all over. Pauline didn't want to fly with me. I took her up a couple of times. But, usually, she'd beg off. She was an adventurous gal, but she didn't want to fly with me. I don't know why. I took a lot of other people up. There were several guys who worked with me who liked to fly, and I flew with some other pilots in the club. I went all the way down to the southern end of Japan. I flew up north during the winter when the snow was way high. It was kind of neat flying in there and landing with these snow banks piled high by the runway. I landed at American military bases most of the time. I flew over the Bay of Tokyo. I flew over where the old prisoner of war camps had been during the war. Most all the prison camps had been obliterated by that time. But, still, I could almost feel something about those places from the air. The horrible things that went on down there for our guys.

From audio recordings made on October 10, 2009 and June 23, 2010.

It Was Just a Bare Skeleton

In that hanger at the flying club they had an L-5. That's
an old military plane, a single engine. It was an observation
plane that the military used for going over enemy territory
to photograph the land and stuff like that. It would lift off
in 300 feet if you really had to get off that quick. By this
time, though, it was just a bare skeleton, sitting over there
in the corner. I asked the president of the club, "What are
you going to do with that L-5?"

"The Boy Scouts are working on it."

"I've never seen a Boy Scout near that thing."

"Well, what do you want to do with it?"

"I want to rebuild it and fly it."

"You'd have to buy it."

"All right, I'll buy it."

"I'll put it up to the committee for a vote."

So the board of the club voted and the president came up
to me one day and said, "It's approved. You can buy that
plane. How much do you want to pay for it?"

We started knocking figures around. I said, "I'll give you
$900 for it."

"You know you get a new engine with it."

"You're kidding."

"There's one in that crate over there. You want to up
that price a little?"

"How many people want to buy it?"

"You're the only one."

"Well, then leave it at $900."

He took that number to the committee and they said,
"Oh, give it to him for $900."

So, I bought the airplane and I started working on it. I
started with the wings. It had fabric wings stretched over
wood. There were five or six wings lying there. I picked out
the best ones and then went to work.

We had an IA inspector, who inspected all of the club's
aircraft, and he could inspect and sign off my work on the

plane. I'd be over there working on it until nine or ten o'clock at night. They'd holler, "We're going to turn off the lights. Are you about done?"

This went on for awhile, and I started thinking there wasn't any reason for me to keep coming over to the hangar to work on it. I decided to take the plane over to Totsuka, where I was stationed. There was a building there that had a basketball court in it. Nobody ever played basketball. I went to the skipper and asked him if I could put my airplane on the basketball court.

"Well, what if someone wants to play basketball?"

"We can just shove the plane into the corner."

So, he gave me permission to work on it in there. I loaded the plane up on a trailer and pulled it behind a Navy pickup truck to Totsuka. It was about fifteen miles. It didn't have the wings on it, but it was still quite a sight, that plane rolling through the streets of Japan.

I moved everything onto the basketball court. I spread out and turned it into a regular workshop. It's a good thing nobody wanted to play basketball, because my stuff was pretty well scattered all over the place. I finally got the wings built. Then I worked on the fuselage. It was made out of welded steel tubing. Every time I finished part of the plane, the inspector came over and signed it off. It was quite a process to make the plane safe. Then I worked on the wheels and the brakes. Then I pulled the new engine out of the crate and put it in there.

Time was running out. It was almost getting time for me to leave Japan. I had orders to join MCB 4 in Port Hueneme, California. I wrote the command and asked for an extension of six months so I could finish my airplane. They gave me my extension. I finally got the plane all put together. I rebuilt the whole thing from start to finish and it passed all the inspections. I got a twenty foot can, one of these big, long containers. I put the plane in there and that's the way it was shipped back to the States.

From an audio recording made on October 10, 2009.

That Sucker Flew Like an Angel

We packed up and left Japan. I made my way over to Oxnard, California, which is where Port Hueneme is. I went over to the Oxnard Airport. There was an old Marine there running a flying club. So, I went in and talked to him.

"I got this airplane coming over from Japan. It's an L-5."

"Oh, I flew one of them." He had been an enlisted Marine pilot. The Marines used to allow enlisted men to be pilots, before they went to officers only for pilots.

He said, "Tell you what. If you want to leave your airplane here, you can. I'll take good care of it. I'll go down to Long Beach and pick it up on my trailer for you."

When the plane arrived, he went down and got it for me. We started working on it together and got the wings on. I put the prop on and the cowling on the engine. We got it all hooked up and put together. He was an inspector, so he could sign off on it. We fired that sucker up, and, boy, that engine just revved up like new. I wanted to fly it before I was deployed to Puerto Rico.

So, one day I was out there firing that engine up. I had to put a certain amount of time on the engine before I flew it because it was a rebuilt engine. I was out there in the plane sitting pretty close to his office. I read in the manual that you were supposed to run the engine up to 1,500 rpms and then drop it back down. I did that over and over. Well, he got tired of listening to that crap. He came out there and hollered, "Cut that engine off!"

"What's the problem?"

"Now look," he said. "I already signed off on that airplane. Take it over there to the tower and put it out on the runway and you fly it."

"Good!" I was ready.

I had gas in the tank. I was all set. I did exactly what he said. I had the radio working so I contacted the tower and I gave him my call sign.

"Request permission for takeoff."

I had never flown that sucker. I didn't know what to expect with the weight and balance. I thought, well, here goes. I knew what I was doing, but I was a little apprehensive. I just eased the throttle forward; she really wanted to fly. I kept easing up and finally I hauled that stick back just a little bit and I flew on down the runway and I took her up. That sucker flew like an angel. I didn't know where I was going. So, I just flew along the coast. I went way north in California. I made a couple landings at this little airport about 200 miles from Oxnard. Then I brought her back home and landed. The old Marine sergeant came out there.

"Wow," he said. "You did it."

From an audio recording made on October 10, 2009.

Working on the L-5 on the basketball court in Japan

Like Shooting a Cannon

In Port Hueneme I joined up with MCB 4. The battalion had just gotten back from a deployment to Spain. I was a company chief. I had about 130 men in my company. I took care of all the bitching and growling, petty stuff with the men in my company. We were there about a year before our deployment to Puerto Rico. We trained and trained and trained some more. We did lots of cross-training on all the different trades. And, we went to the rifle range a lot. I learned to use a lot of weapons that I hadn't used before. I made marksman, again. We did one round of training with .45 handguns. You can't be all that accurate with a .45. That sucker would rock back up in the air; it was almost like shooting a cannon. Whoom.

One time they took us way up in the mountains, north of San Francisco into the snow belt. There was a Marine training station up there. They set up all kinds of attack plans. We had to defend our position because the Marines were trying to take us out. The Marines would come sneaking in there during the night and overrun us Seabees. We weren't quite as stealthy as they were. It was brutal out there. The snow was chest deep. One night I set up the defenses for my company as best as I could. Man, it was cold. It was about sixteen degrees below zero that night. The guys were huddled up together trying to keep from freezing to death. A couple of my guys went into hypothermia; we had to get them out of there. I had a lot of things going on that night that kept me from walking the lines and making sure everybody was awake and doing their jobs. We got along great and held them off until about three o'clock in the morning. Then the Marines came roaring through our lines. The company commander was wiped out. "Why did you let them come through your line?" he hollered at me.

"I couldn't keep them out of there. Half of my guys were asleep and the other half were nearly frozen to death."

I thought we did good, but this commander didn't. I don't know why the hell we had to train in the snow. We were getting ready to go to Puerto Rico. We all asked the same question. Why can't we train in Hawaii where the conditions were more like Puerto Rico? That's the Navy.

Still, it was all good training.

From an audio recording made on August 11, 2011.

Money Wasn't the Object

Eventually, the whole battalion, 600 men, went to Roosevelt Roads, Puerto Rico. Our main project was working on Waves quarters; that's for women sailors. Mostly, the buildings were already up. We had to do all of the interior work. My company went to work putting in all the plumbing. The company commander would tell me what we needed to do and then I assigned duties to the men and checked up on them. I didn't do much of the physical work myself. I did a lot of paperwork at the company headquarters, though.

They had a flight club in Puerto Rico, and, of course, I joined it right away. I flew a lot with a Navy jet pilot. He taught me a lot of things about tricky landings, with cross winds and little landing strips. Some of those landing strips around the island looked just like little toothpicks down there.

The flying club had two or three Cessna 172s and those would hold three passengers. Before long, I started hauling people over to St. Thomas and St. Croix on the weekends. Most of them were other chiefs. I didn't charge anything for this taxi service. I would fly people out on Friday night. Everybody would put life jackets on because we were flying over water all the way. I'd fly them over, drop them off, and fly back and pick up three more people. I just asked them to pay for the gas. They'd be at the airport on Sunday afternoon for the pickup and I'd fly them back home. That gave me a lot of over the water flying time. I'd fly people around the island, too. If they'd pay for the gas, I'd take them. I wanted the flight time and there were always people eager to go.

I was in Puerto Rico about a year. Pauline came down after a few months. I rented a nice apartment for her right there in San Juan. I stayed out at the base most of the time during the week.

Things weren't going so great on the job, though. There was competition between me and this other chief. He didn't like the way I was handling a couple of the job sites. This chief kept bad-mouthing me. He thought he could do a better job than me, things like that. It was just a bunch of animosity between him and me. It got pretty deep. Finally, I got tired of it all. I told the company commander, "I can't handle this anymore. I think I'll retire."

"Oh, you can't," he said. "You've got to go with us to our next deployment. We're going to Diego Garcia over in the Indian Ocean."

"I'm going to tell you, commander, I've seen every crap hole in the Pacific. I've been to some real dandy places. I'm not interested in going to Diego Garcia. If I have to retire to put a stop to this nonsense with this other chief, I will."

"But, you're our physical education advisor. Who would handle that if you leave?"

Physical education advisor. Hell, all that meant was I lined up the troops and did calisthenics with them, and I was pretty good at it. I could do all the jumps and squats with the young guys. He wanted me to stay. I wasn't a bad chief. I was a good chief.

I said, "No, I think it's time for me to retire."

"Put your papers in if you want to, but why don't you take over special services in the meantime? We need someone to be our recreation coordinator. These guys lay around here on the weekends, either smoking pot or drinking too much. I'll give you a truck and an office. You can go all over the island and pick spots where these guys can go for the weekend. I'll give you a bus, and I'll pay for the food."

"That sounds fine, skipper." That's how I became a full-time travel agent in Puerto Rico. I went to every corner of that island looking for places to take these guys on the weekends. It all worked out fine, once I got my feet wet. I was the weekend recreation chairman. That was my duty, to get those guys out of the barracks and on the road. I went to San Juan and talked to travel agents. They told me about

195

different towns and cities. I took my truck out on my own and scouted out these out-of-the-way places.

When I got something set up, I'd make posters to advertise it. I had to use my imagination. I put the posters up on the bulletin boards the week before the outing. One time I drew a bus and had all these sailors hanging out of the windows. I'd make the posters big so everybody could see them. This was a way to sharpen their appetites for a little travel. The guys had to come and sign up in my office. Most of these guys didn't have any money. They always blew it on something. So, I tried to keep everything real cheap. We'd stay at these little hotels if there were any in the area. We'd set up tents if we had to. I usually had forty or fifty guys sign up each weekend; some would bring their wives with them. The women would cook for us sometimes.

The first place we went was one of those bays where these tiny animals glow at night. Boy, I tell you, we got those guys out there that night and they saw the water glowing. They really thought that was something.

Whenever we went to the east end of the island, we brought along sleeping bags and stayed in some barracks at an old air base. I tried to do stuff like that to keep the guys from spending too much money.

We went to the town of Arecibo. There were some caves there that had been inhabited by some early Indians. Those were some real interesting cave paintings that we saw. One time we went to some drag races. That was pretty exciting. We set up our tents next to the drag strip. We usually only stayed out one night. The guys went willingly. We didn't force them. I had to make it interesting. It all worked out.

Then one day the commander called me into his office. "Your retirement papers are ready," he said. "You're going back to the States."

I felt kind of sorry that I put in for retirement. I thought about pulling them. I talked it over with Pauline.

"What are we going to do?" I asked her.

"I don't know," she said. "You were gung ho for getting out. Personally, I like the Navy. I'd rather you stay in."

"Well, I like to fly airplanes. Maybe I'll start us a little business somewhere."

"I don't really want you to leave the Navy."

"I got my time in. Why not?"

I figured, no, that's enough. I don't know why I retired like I did. It wasn't the men or the work. I guess it was the politics, pure and simple. The politics in that battalion drove me wild. I knew I could find something to do after the Navy. So, I went back to Oxnard. I took my papers over to the personnel office and they put me in the fleet reserve for a few years. I ended up with thirty years in the Navy. When I turned in my papers I thought, my God, I made it. I survived.

Looking back over the whole time in the Navy, I really tried to keep our country safe. That was my motivation. I was in the Navy back in the days when I didn't get much money for it. Money wasn't the object. I did it because I love my country. If someone tried to invade this land and take over our country today, old veterans like me who couldn't stand for it would probably have to die. Die trying to save the country.

From audio recordings made on October 11, 2009, February 5, 2010, June 13, 2011, and August 11, 2011.

PART VIII
NEW BEGINNINGS
1980 - PRESENT

*"Anything you want to do in life,
you just do it, crazy or not."*

The Head of My Class

We went back to Oxnard. I turned in my retirement papers and picked up my airplane. This was 1979. We headed back to Corpus Christi where we still had our house on the Laguna Madre. Pauline drove our little VW and I flew the L-5. She'd meet me at little airports along the way.

I decided I wanted to go to aviation maintenance school. I checked around and found there was a school in Houston. I took advantage of the GI bill which paid for the school. I earned that benefit, so I figured I'd take it.

It was a year and a half course. That was a tough phase of my life. Here was this dude with an eighth grade education. I was fifty-six years old, thirty years older than everyone else in the class. Some of those young guys in the class were smart-alecks and didn't really care about studying hard. I told myself, I'm not going in here to make mediocre grades. I'm going to give it everything I can. I'd get up at four o'clock in the morning and hit those books, especially on test days.

They packed this math on me. It was pretty rough at first. I'd never been to high school. I never learned algebra and trigonometry. I thought, what do I need with trig? But, I had to learn it. I studied hard. When I finished the school, I was the head of my class. I got my federal certifications for two areas of small aircraft mechanics, airframe and power plant. That means I could work on the body of an airplane and on the engine. I still have my diploma hanging on the wall. I'm pretty proud of that.

From audio recordings made on October 10, 2009, October 11, 2009, June 23, 2010, and August 11, 2011.

199

It Wasn't Crazy

While I was still going to school, I said to Pauline, "They're selling property out there in Waller."

"Waller? We don't need to buy that property. I'm not going to live all the way out there and drive back and forth to Houston."

Waller is a little town about forty miles northwest of Houston. I was interested in these two lots because they were right next to a little airport. I figured I could start my own little aircraft maintenance business there.

I won that argument and we bought two lots for $15,000. One was a commercial lot and the other was a regular lot. That meant I could build a hanger to service airplanes on the commercial lot, and I could build a house on the other lot. I told Pauline, "We'll get it built up and then after awhile, we can sell it and we can live wherever you want." That was the plan.

I was still going to school when I started building our house and a hanger for this business I wanted to start. I did this all by myself. It was crazy. Well, it wasn't crazy, either. Anything you want to do in life, you just do it, crazy or not.

I went out there every weekend and worked. I started building on the residential lot. I built a big, open storage unit, sort of like a hanger, where I could store a couple of derelict airplanes that I was planning to rebuild. I set up some living quarters in there, too. I put in a set of bunk beds and a little kitchen and a bathroom. When I was out there working on the house, the natives, the local people, came around there all worried that I was going to ruin the neighborhood.

"What are you doing?" they asked.

"I'm building a hanger."

"You can't do that."

"Watch me."

Those people were getting redder and redder when they realized I wasn't going to budge. They thought I was putting up a piece of junk. They didn't like me putting up a storage unit on that lot. I knew it would look fine when I was finished with it. They hassled me for awhile and finally Pauline said, "You better leave him alone. You're making him mad."

I said, "I don't want to come down off this ladder with this hammer. Pack up your little butts and head out."

They got the message.

I kept working on that hanger in stages. I eventually built a second story on it. We had an upstairs living area, with a balcony. We had quite a view of the airport. There were parachutists who were jumping there, too. We'd watch those planes take off and go up to 10,000 feet and they'd kick out these parachutists and they'd come floating down. Some of them landed in the lake once in awhile.

After I got my first storage unit done with some living quarters in it, I started on my big hanger, a sixty by sixty hanger. I ordered up a bunch of twelve inch steel I-beams. I bought this old Allis-Chalmers tractor, a great big old thing with one wheel in the front and two wheels in the back. There was a little scoop bucket on the front. I extended out the scoop by adding some skids, like long arms, so I could put these I-beams on them. I'd scoop up an I-beam onto the tractor and lift it up into place. Then, I'd jump off the tractor and run up a ladder next to the I-beam and whack a few welds on it. That's how I got those big beams put up. The hanger was about eleven feet tall at the door, sixteen feet at the peak. It was a big thing. After awhile, I built another hanger, a forty by forty. Everything turned out all right.

After I finished school, we moved out there and I started my business. It was a good business. People brought their airplanes to me for annual inspections. I would keep the plane for two or three days checking everything that I was certified to do. Then my neighbor across the street would come and finish the inspection. He was rated an IA, which was an inspection authorization, one rate higher than my A&P. I also did maintenance and general repair work on

201

planes. I made a good living and I enjoyed what I did. Sometimes, when I had the space, I would hanger airplanes, too. I could put two or three planes in my big hanger and I had room outside to tie them down, too. I'd charge $100 a month rent for storage. Most of the airplanes that I stored were for weekend pilots. You'd think all these guys that had airplanes would be real honest fellows. Well, some of them were pretty crafty.

One guy, who was pretty well-known around town, came and said, "I'm taking my airplane out of the hanger."

"You put the money in my hand that you owe me, and then you can take it."

He got all huffy. Man, he was torn up. "I'm going to get the sheriff."

"Go ahead. I'm sure he'd like to hear your story of why you haven't paid your rent for almost a year." He didn't do it.

That night I was in bed and I heard the hanger doors sliding open. I went down there with my pistol. Here was this same guy.

"What are you doing?" I said.

"I'm leaving on a trip."

"Not until you pay me. We've already gone through this."

He backed off. He knew I was in the right.

"Bring the money tomorrow and you can have the airplane." So he left, and then I took the propeller off of his plane and hid it. He wasn't going anywhere in that plane. Finally, he came around with the money and I put his prop back on. You'd think these people, well-known in the community, would have a pretty good stash of cash. Some people are always out to slip it to you if they can.

From audio recordings made on June 23, 2010, February 17, 2011, August 11, 2011, and September 15, 2011.

Crooked as a Dog's Hind Leg

When we first moved to Waller, that whole area around the airport was clean as a pip. Then a drug runner came in there. I can't remember his name, and I wouldn't want to know it anymore, anyway. He and his gang started making flights in and out of our little airport, loaded with drugs. They had a high performance plane. They'd come in at night. They'd fly in right past our porch. Our house was right on the taxiway. If they went to a hanger at the other end of the field, I didn't see what they were doing. But a lot of times they pulled up to a hanger close to my house. I could look right out of my bedroom window and watch them unload marijuana by the tons. As soon as the plane landed, they'd have it unloaded pretty quick. They were running one or two flights in there every week. I talked it over with my neighbor.

"We got some drug runners," I told him. "I saw them down there last night and they were unloading those drugs like mad. What should we do? We can't let that go on."

"I'll call the sheriff." Well, this sheriff was as crooked as a dog's hind leg. He didn't do anything. He was probably in on the whole thing.

My neighbor finally convinced the feds, the Drug Enforcement people, that this was going on. One night, Pauline and I were in our little bridal suite, that's what we used to call it, our quarters above my hanger. We were up there and I saw this plane come in and land. I knew it was the drug runners. Then all of a sudden, all of these big flood lights came on. The feds were out there waiting for them. They hollered, "Everybody down on the ground." Man, those drug runners scattered like scared rabbits. But, the feds had them ringed and collected all of them. They carted them off and packed up the marijuana and cocaine.

I said to Pauline, "We won't see those guys for awhile."

"Good riddance."

203

The next day, we were out in the yard and this pickup came roaring by. All these drug runners that they had arrested the night before were hanging out of their truck waving at us. They were back out there at the airport within twenty-four hours. These guys were serious; they had shotguns in their trucks, and we always wondered if they would retaliate against us for turning them in. But, they never could pinpoint exactly who turned them in. It was scary.

The local people or the feds would arrest them every now and then. It was really a waste to call the sheriff; he was just as bad as they were. That crooked sheriff was killed in a car accident. They said he drove off the road. I don't believe that. I think those drug runners shoved him off the road. They did him in.

When the drug runners moved in, a lot of people moved out. Like a dummy, I stayed there. If I'd have put a fence around my place, that might have been better. Made us feel a little more secure. This went on for years until I finally sold the place. It really put a damper on my nice business that I had going.

From audio recordings made on October 11, 2009 and June 23, 2010.

Everything Changed for Me

Pauline and I decided to take a trip back to Japan. Since I was retired from the Navy, we could fly on military planes just about anywhere in the world, if they had space available. We knew we could catch an Air Force transport from Seattle over to Japan, so we headed up to Washington. On the way there Pauline started complaining that her right breast was hurting. The pain wouldn't go away, so when we got up to Tacoma we went to the Madigan Army Medical Center there. They took a bunch of tests and discovered she had breast cancer. They didn't mess around; they operated right away and took off her breast.

Of course, we didn't go to Japan. We turned around, when she was recovered enough from the surgery, and went back to Texas. We went over to Brooke Army Medical Center in San Antonio to start her treatments. They were real reassuring. "We'll have her out of here in no time, good as new." They did lots more tests and started her on that chemotherapy. She suffered from that. It would bring tears to my eyes. They didn't have the treatments back then in the early 1980s that they do now. She was such a brave woman. She kept working, too. She was still driving back and forth from Waller to her job in Houston. I told her to quit her job, but she didn't want to.

It was a constant battle for three years and I fought right along with her. The cancer was spreading. She knew she wasn't going to make it. We went back to San Antonio for the last treatment. She didn't even know she was in the car. She was so weak. I couldn't get her out of the car and I couldn't carry her by myself. I went into that hospital trying to get someone's attention. I pounded on the desk and yelled, "Somebody's got to help me! Bring me a wheelchair for my wife!"

A person came over to me and said, "Now, listen, you can't go around here banging on tables like that."

"You listen. My wife is in the car dying. She could go any minute. Get me some help."

Finally, they rounded up an orderly with a wheelchair and we went out and brought Pauline into the hospital. They admitted her and she rallied a little bit.

"My God, Paulie," I said, "I think we might whip this thing yet."

"Irvin, bring me some strawberries. I really would like some juicy strawberries."

I went out and bought the biggest, most beautiful strawberries that I could find. I washed those things until hell wouldn't have them, they were that clean. I took those strawberries into her hospital room and, man, she sure enjoyed eating them. She died a couple of days later on April 4, 1986. I've always wondered if there was something about those strawberries. Maybe I shouldn't have given them to her. I took her back home to Ohio and buried her next to her father. Everything changed for me after she died.

She was quite a gal. One in a million. She wasn't a raving beauty, but she had lots of beauty about her. We had our differences like most couples, but we worked it out. Nothing really dramatic. We were good buddies. We enjoyed each other. It was a steady love affair. We were together for thirty-three years.

For many years Paulie and I had driven between our places in Corpus Christi and Waller. We usually took the same route all the time. After she was gone, I drove that normal route and I went by these places where we used to stop and have lunch. We'd laugh and giggle about silly things. I had to start taking a different route. It took a long time to stop the memories from hurting. I really loved Pauline.

From audio recordings made on March 26, 2009, February 18, 2011, and August 10, 2011.

I Kept Running

The night that Pauline died is when I started running. I went to the motel that night and I couldn't sleep. I went outside and ran and ran. I ran all night long, just up and down the streets. I'd always been a bit of a runner. I ran in the military for training, of course. I had always managed to get out and run a few miles whenever I could. I used to take my whole company out for long runs in California and Puerto Rico in our combat boots. After the Navy, I still ran occasionally, but not very seriously.

After Pauline died, I went down to our house in Corpus Christi and started working on it. I was cleaning it up to get it ready to rent out again. One of my neighbors down there was a runner. He ran marathons and he entered those Ironman competitions, too. When he went out in the mornings to run, I started going along with him. I ran at first trying to get everything off my shoulders. Pauline's long illness and death.

"Why don't you run a 5k or a 10k," he said. "Those are easy to start with."

I kept running and I did what he said. I started entering these little runs, a 5k here and a 10k there. I found I was pretty good at it. I could run a 10k real easy. I'd usually do a 9 minute mile in a 10k. I ran every day. I'd get up at 5:30 every morning and knock out five or six miles. After I started running, I couldn't stop. I enjoyed it very much. It was bringing me back to life after Pauline died.

One day, I said to myself, I can run a marathon. It's just twenty-six miles. If I can run ten miles every day, I can surely run twenty-six miles. So, when I was sixty-three years old, I ran my first marathon. It was the Houston Tenneco. It took me almost five hours to finish it. There were a few runners who were crapping out close to the finish. I stopped and encouraged them to get their butts in gear and get on with it.

207

"You're so close. Don't give up now," I told them. They had worked awfully hard to get where they were and I hated to see them fall short. I helped this one young lady cross the finish line. I expect I could have made it in about four hours and forty minutes if I hadn't stopped. For my first marathon, I thought that was pretty good.

Running a marathon takes a lot of determination. I'd think about getting to the next mile post, the next water stop. I'd grab those cups of water and gulp one down and dump another one over my head. I'd feel better and think, well, I can handle the next mile. That's how I got through them, one mile at a time. After a few tries and good training, I could run an 8.5 minute mile pretty consistently in marathons.

Whenever I ran a marathon, or any race, I used to always look over the competition before that starting gun went off. I'd look for older guys who were probably in my age bracket. One time I was running in the Blue Bell 10k. I saw this guy who looked over sixty and he had slim legs, as skinny as fence posts. I figured he was a real runner. I thought, well, I've got to get ahead of this guy early, if I want to win my division. We started out and I popped off at a pretty good pace. I got pretty far ahead of this guy. I got to a long hill and I could hear this heavy breathing behind me. It was this guy with the fence post legs. An old racer had told me, "Whenever you've got a real problem with another runner, catch him on the hill." Well, that's pretty good advice. Old fence posts must have been told the same thing by somebody because he eased ahead of me going up that hill. So, I put on a couple extra knots of speed. I eased ahead of him. We were still on the hill and I was getting a few yards ahead of him. Slap, slap, slap, I could hear him coming up behind me again. He had to work awful hard to get ahead of me and I had to work awful hard to be a real competitor to him. I heard that sucker breathing behind me and he went past me again. It was only about half a mile to the finish line once we got to the top of that hill. I thought to myself, I'll wait until I get forty or fifty yards from the finish line and then I'll pop on everything I got. He was thinking the same thing I was. He just weaseled ahead of me through that darn gate. He finished first and I finished second in our age group.

I think altogether I ran ten marathons and a whole bunch of other shorter races. I always enjoyed it up until the last marathon. Toward the end of that marathon, I had to run up a steep hill. About a mile before the end, I was feeling pretty tired. I thought, this isn't so much fun anymore. If it wasn't fun, I didn't want to do it anymore. I figured I could still enjoy running just as much on my own. I ran my last marathon in 1995 when I was seventy-one years old.

From audio recordings made on March 26, 2009 and September 15, 2011.

I Got Rolled

I'd read a bunch of reports, and I'd seen a couple of programs on television about the Amazon forest being cut down for wood. I thought to myself, I've never been there and I don't want to miss the chance of seeing the forest there and the Amazon waters. So, I conjured up a trip down the Oronoco River with the intent to go down all the way to the Amazon. I checked on the airlines and found that I could fly into Caracas, Venezuela. From there I could fly down to a city called San Fernando de Atabapo. It's the last city on this road in Venezuela. I booked my flight and flew down there from Houston. I went by myself. I definitely wanted to see that part of the world.

I got down there and planned to be there two months. I stayed about a month. Ran out of money, actually, because I got rolled. When I first got to Caracas, I left my money in the hotel room. I locked the door and went down to the swimming pool. I thought, I can watch my room from the pool. Evidently, they were slicker than I was. As soon as this thief saw me dive into the pool and go under the water, he made a run on my billfold. He didn't take my credit card, just my money. I was lucky that I had put most of my money in the safe when I checked into the hotel. So, he didn't get it all. But, it sure made things tough for me. I went all over Caracas and saw the city.

Then I flew down to San Fernando and stayed at a little hotel. The floor in my room had been painted red with this cheap red paint. Man, I'd walk out of my room with half the floor's paint on the bottom of my shoes. They were good people there at that hotel and my stay was enjoyable.

I started asking a few people around town where I could find a guide who could take me all the way to Brazil. I finally ran into a guy who was a tour guide of sorts and a game hunter, too. He was a native. He spoke good English, though. There were two or three other people in town who wanted to go down the Oronoco River and go into Brazil and see the Amazon. I was hoping to go down the river toward the Atlantic. But, it didn't work out quite that way.

So, this fellow said, "Yeah, I can take you down there. I got a couple of other people who want to go, too. We'll drive about a hundred miles into the forest, back to this ranch where we'll stop and eat. Then we'll go down to where there's a guy with a boat."

Two of the people chickened out and that left me with this other guy from Detroit. He was going to pay the guide half and I'd pay half. We went down to this big *rancho* where we had lunch. They raised beef cattle there. They would butcher a cow and hang the meat in an airplane and fly it out of there to town.

We then made contact with this guy who had the boat. My God, he lived out in the real wilderness with his wife and two little daughters. They were in the middle of nowhere. He made his living on the river. He hunted alligators and that sort of thing. He agreed to take us all the way to the end of the Oronoco River. He said he could show us the Indian villages. Primitive villages where not many tourists went.

Me and this fellow from Detroit climbed into the boat with this guy and off we went. It was just a little open boat with a motor on the back. Going down the river with rain forest all around was nice and peaceful. Although, it wasn't thick forest everywhere. It was pretty sparse in some areas. The guide brought some food along and we fished, too. He cooked the fish over a little fire beside the river. He took good care of us. We slept out in the open at night. We had hammocks, tied them up in the trees. We saw monkeys hanging in the trees, a couple of howler monkeys, too. Boy, they could make a racket.

As we got further down the river, our guide pulled up into these villages so we could visit the natives. The villages were very unique, just like they were 500 years ago. The people lived in huts, cone-shaped huts, with no electricity. We went in a few of their huts. They had seen other tourists before, so they weren't totally surprised to see us. Those

211

Indians were fantastic. Then ran around with nothing on, practically. Just little loincloths. We couldn't really talk to them. They had their own dialects. They didn't try to smother us with things to buy. They had some flutes that they had made. I bought a couple of carvings of Jesus on the cross. Missionaries had been through there, apparently. Then we retraced our steps back to the ranch. The first guy came and picked us up. That trip down the river took about a week and a half.

I stayed around San Fernando for awhile. Just hanging out. There weren't any other Americans around town most of the time. I was a runner then, so I went out running every day. I ran a few times with the Venezuelan Army. They were out training. Running around in that country was kind of hairy at times. One day I was out running. I'd run all the way out of town a few miles and I got to the river, turned around and started back. All of a sudden, I looked up and there was this big black panther. I stopped right in my tracks. I thought, well, I'm not going any farther; I'll just wait to see what he does. He walked across the road right in front of me and into the forest. I didn't know if he was lying in wait behind a tree to jump out at me when I went by him or not. I went by there as quick as I could. He didn't seem to care about me. I probably wouldn't have been good eating for him.

San Fernando was a nice town, although a little primitive. There was live music at night, sometimes. There was a little central plaza and people would gather at night, wham on their guitars and sing. When I was very young, I learned a couple of Spanish songs, so I sang, too. They really liked that; I wasn't just an old tourist rolling through town. They were good people.

I decided I needed to head back home. I had less than $50 cash left. So I went back to the airport in Caracas. I had some time to kill before my flight so I went up to this veranda at the airport. It was like a big observation deck. I noticed these characters watching me. Believe me, they were characters. I was real tired. I decided to stretch out on the bench there and take a nap. I had bought a *cuatro* guitar, one with four strings. I had my backpack and my guitar with me. I leaned back on the bench with my backpack underneath me and my guitar in my arms. Darned if they didn't steal my guitar while I was sleeping. I had ahold of that sucker, too. How they got it out of my arms, I don't know. These were very tricky fellows. There was a batch of thieves there.

I never was totally satisfied with that trip; I didn't go as far as I wanted to go on the Amazon River. If I hadn't had bad luck getting my money stolen right at the first, I could have done more. That trip down the river was smooth, though. Seeing all of the natives and going into the villages. That made the trip worthwhile.

From audio recordings made on June 21, 2010, August 10, 2011, and August 16, 2011.

I Enjoyed Being with Her

About five years after Pauline had died, I guess I got lonely. I started driving into Houston to this Methodist Church. I liked this church. They had a singles study group. I started going to that. There was a pretty, young, blond-headed woman in this study group, too. Her name was Eunice. She worked in a bank as a head teller. She was in charge of the drive-thru. She was very good at her job. She had gone through a divorce and had a teenage son. We started talking to each other at the study group. This group also helped out at the Salvation Army, with their meal programs. So, we'd see each other there. She was in charge of the bookwork and they hit me up to do the dishes.

"Can you wash up the pots and pans?"

"Boy, that's right down my alley." They taught me how to wash pots and pans on the *Gudgeon*. I was a Brock-trained man. So, that's how it started. We'd see each other at church and at the Salvation Army. Then one day I asked her, "Why don't you come out to Waller? I'm going to be flying my airplane this weekend. Would you like to go for a ride?" That sounded fine to her.

We got to going together. I enjoyed being with her. It was pretty casual. Then, she had to leave her apartment, so she came out to Waller to live with me. I didn't think there was anything wrong with that arrangement. That's just how it was. I helped her through some things with her son. Teen-agers, well, they can get into trouble all kinds of ways. I told him, "You got to knock this crap off." He's a wonderful guy now, has a good job and a family.

One day I said, "Eunice, if you want to get married, that will be all right with me." It wasn't really much of a pro-posal. After we got married, she kept her job for awhile. But, she gave it up and started on adventures with me.

From audio recordings made on October 11, 2009 and August 10, 2011.

I'm Going to Throw Everything Out

Eunice and I decided to fly around and see some sights in some western states. So, we piled into my Cessna with our big dog, Bear. We took along all kinds of camping equipment, a tent, a couple of stoves, sleeping bags, and other stuff. All that gear was pretty heavy, but the Cessna could handle it. I liked camping out. Eunice didn't care all that much for camping, but she was a good sport about it.

We flew all over, setting down at little airstrips. We'd rent a car and go sightseeing for a few days. We went all over the Dakotas. We stopped at Mount Rushmore. We went up to Wyoming, down through Utah and Arizona. We were leisurely taking our time, just looking over the country. When we camped out, we just pitched our tent right there at those little airports. We'd been gone about three weeks and Eunice said, "Why don't we start home?"

"Okay," I said, "but, I want to go down to Bisbee, Arizona first." I wanted to see the big open pit copper mine they had down there. So, we flew on down to Bisbee which is pretty close to the Mexican border. We were there awhile and then we fueled up and headed for El Paso. Well, we ran into real bad weather. Big thunderstorms. I was trying to dodge around these darn thunderstorms. We made so many turns, I wasn't quite sure where we were. None of my instruments were working worth a darn. We kept going, but I was getting leery about running out of gas. We were toddling along and I said, "Eunie, I've got no idea where we are. If you see anything that looks like a town or an airstrip, holler."

So, we were both on the lookout, and we spotted what looked like a little airport down there. There were two airstrips and a ranch house close by, and it looked like a pretty up-to-date place. I made a big turn around and looked over the airstrip. I could see some cracks in the runway. I thought, well, that's just the way it is. I picked the smaller strip. The other strip didn't look quite right to me. The two strips were lying there kind of like a T. Anyway, I set the Cessna down. It was a bit of a rough landing, but passable. We climbed out of the airplane and pulled the dog out, too. I said, "Let's go on up to the ranch house and talk to these people."

We had to walk through this thick mesquite that was all around the runway to get to the house. It was probably a quarter of a mile to the ranch house. There were a bunch of mangy looking cows with big, old, long horns trying to graze around that mesquite. But they didn't look like Texas longhorns. It suddenly dawned on me, "I think we're in Mexico."

When we got to the gate by the house I said to Eunice, "Stay back. I'll go up there myself." I was starting to think, something's wrong here. Two ranch hands came out of the house. I tried to talk to them in my wimpy Spanish.

"*Donde*, El Paso?"

One fellow pointed north, but he wasn't very friendly.

I said, "*Sí, muchisimas gracias. Adiós.*" I turned around and hightailed it back to Eunice.

"Get your butt up there and move! Let's go. This isn't the right place for us." I figured this place was for drug runners.

"What's the matter?" Eunice said.

"Let's just get going."

I was a runner in those days and I took out. I was loping too fast for Eunice. I hollered back at her, "If you want to live, sweetie, keep up with me!"

We had to go under a barbed wire fence and wrestle our way through that damn thick mesquite. I was anxious to get out of there. I kept expecting to see those dudes come up there in a Jeep after us. I was worried they might kill us to get the airplane. Who would ever know what happened to us? I had a 30-30 in the back of the airplane, but I figured that would be no match for whatever weapons they had.

We finally made it back to the airplane. Our clothes were ripped to heck from that mesquite and we were bleeding from cuts all over. We dove into the airplane and I fired it

216

up. I taxied up to the far end of the strip. That mesquite was just like a wall, six or eight feet high. I could see the runway but I couldn't see over the mesquite. I wound up that little old Cessna.

"Here we go, Eunice. Hang on."

I started down the runway. Just about the time I was ready to take off I hit those ruts and lost twenty knots, just like that. I couldn't avoid the ruts by going on the edge of the runway because that mesquite came right up to the edge. It was a real ticklish situation. I knew I wasn't going to be able to make that first pass. There was no wind sock, so I didn't know which way the wind was blowing. When we got to the end of the runway, I decided to turn and try it back the other way. All this time, I'm thinking, boy, they're going to come out to this airstrip after us and what the hell am I going to do? I knew this was a bad, bad place to be.

We went down the runway the other way. Same thing happened, I kept hitting those ruts. I realized that somebody had probably come in there and cut these runways up to stop the drug traffic. I had seen those ruts from the air and I should have never gone in there. I thought it was a ranch. Well, it was. It was a drug ranch. We got to the other end of the runway. I still wasn't getting enough speed to get that plane up.

"Eunie," I said, "now don't get excited. Take your billfold out of your purse and hold onto it because I'm going to throw everything out of this airplane."

"You're going to do what?"

"I'm throwing everything out to get the weight off this airplane." We had that airplane loaded with clothes and cameras and souvenirs and camping equipment.

"Make sure you've got your credit cards and your driver's license. That's all we're keeping."

That big old heavy dog was sitting back there panting. I looked at her, but, I wouldn't have thrown her out for anything. I thought, well, if we're going to die, all three of us will die together. I turned the plane around again and stopped. I started tossing everything out. Everything just

217

went sailing out of that airplane. The suitcases popped open when I threw them and our clothes floated down onto that mesquite. The camping gear, the stoves, everything. It was going to be like Christmas for those Mexican guys. We didn't save anything. All we kept was what we could put in our pockets.

After we unloaded everything, I had to stop and think. What had I been taught about short field takeoffs? I thought of Charles Lindberg. I remembered that Lindberg had a bad runway when he took off in New York. He couldn't get enough air speed to get that plane off. I remembered he bounced the plane. I thought, that's the ticket. I got back as far as I could on that runway; it wasn't very long, probably 1,200 feet. I put everything I could on that little engine. We went tearing down there and I started to feel those bumps again. I pulled it back a little bit when I came to a bump and that gave me a bounce. On the last bump, I said, "This is it!" I pulled the yoke back and that gave me enough bounce to get us up to about sixty knots of airspeed. The mesquite was like a wall and I knew I had to clear it. I pulled all the juice I could out of that airplane and we sailed up over that wall of mesquite, but we clipped it with our tires. I didn't care about the tires. We were out of there. We kept going north.

I said, "If I have to, I'll set the plane down on Highway 10." I knew we had to cross that big highway. "Keep your eyes open for Highway 10."

We'd been flying about an hour and the fuel gauge was just hanging there right above the E. We flew right over Juarez. Eunice wanted to get out of the airplane in the worst way. "Let's land right there," she said.

"No," I said, "we're going to El Paso." I knew there was a little airport right close to Highway 10. That's where I wanted to put it down. But, we were getting awful low on fuel. Just barely above empty. We saw the highway and flew down along it but I couldn't find that airport. Then I got ahold of El Paso International Airport on the radio.

"Permission to land. We're low on fuel."

"Do you want to declare an emergency?"

"No."

"Where are you?"

"We're right over runway 27." That's when they got panicky. Here we were flying in there with great big planes all around us.

"Permission to land, I got the runway right under me. It's 27."

"Are you low on fuel?"

Hell, yes, we were low on fuel. I'd already told the guy that and here he wanted to chat.

"You want a tractor to pull you in?"

"No, I just want to get her down."

Finally, he said, "Okay. Permission to land." We plopped that little Cessna down and I was so relieved. If I had to make another pass around that runway, we wouldn't have made it. We taxied up to where they told us to park the plane. We climbed out of that plane and man, we were a sight. I was wearing white shorts and they were covered with blood stains. We were dirty; we had rips in our clothes, blood on us. We had no luggage. Nothing. All we had was that big black dog. And nobody said a thing to us. We went to the car rental counter. They rented us a car. We went to a motel, looking like we'd just been in a fight or something. They didn't say a word. It was like everybody looked that way when they came in to rent a room. It was pretty late by this time, but we went to an all night Walmart and bought some clothes and toothbrushes and those kinds of things.

The next morning when we went out to the plane we could tell someone had gone through it with a fine tooth comb. They'd had drug sniffing dogs in it. But, nobody said anything and we were able to take off. When we got home we saw that the tires were full of mesquite thorns. I had to buy all new tires, but it was worth it to get out of Mexico. I tell you, that was a scary maneuver.

From audio recordings made on October 11, 2009 and June 21, 2010.

Like Gambling with Myself

Eunice and I were still living by the airport in Waller. Things kept getting worse with the drug runners. We minded our own business as much as we could. I was never threatened specifically. They never said to me, "Keep your mouth shut or else. We could firebomb this place, you know." But we got the message that we could be targeted if we caused any trouble for them. One fellow who lived by the airport and had a hanger was helping the drug runners. He was a mechanic and he serviced all their planes. Well, his wife was involved with another fellow with a hanger out there. There was a big fight one night. The sheriff came and picked them all up and hauled them to jail. It was just one thing after another. It was kind of a Peyton Place, you might say. I didn't want to leave; I loved that place. The trouble that was going on at that airport forced us to make a decision about getting away from there. I started thinking about getting some land, a little piece of property where I could have some horses. I had always loved horses. I said to Eunice, "Why don't we go to New Mexico and check around there for some property?"

We hooked up a camper behind the truck and went to northern New Mexico. We stayed about a month and looked at various pieces of property. We didn't see anything that suited us. The New Mexico property was so darn expensive. We went back to Waller, but a little while later we came back to New Mexico to look again. People told us, "There's a lot of property over around Trinidad, Colorado. You ought to slip over there and look at it."

"All right. We'll do it."

We went up and over Raton Pass and came down into Trinidad. We saw these signs with lots of big sales on property and acreage. We got with a real estate agent and she said, "I've got just the place for you. Up on top of a beautiful mesa. You can look out over the mountains. It's got grass, but it's not fenced."

"Take us and show us this Garden of Eden." She took us up this road onto the top of a mesa. We got up there and looked out and saw a beautiful, long view of the mountains. We fell in love with it.

"What's the situation with the water?" we asked her.

"There's no water up here. But, there's a big development going in down below this property. As soon as the development gets a little farther along, there's going to be a big water tank right down below you and you can tap into that." She painted a beautiful picture about water. We bought the property in 1994. The promises about the water never materialized. We still have to haul all our water.

We started coming up from Texas and spending a week or so working on the property, getting everything ready to build a house on it. Putting up the fencing, getting electricity out to the place. That sort of thing. We sold the Waller property and moved out to Trinidad and parked our camper way back in the trees. That camper was the end of the line for us; we had no other place to live. We poured the pad for the house in the summer of 1995. We worked right along, Eunice and me. Building the whole house ourselves.

Living in that trailer in Colorado was no fun during the winter. We froze our butts off. The wind kept blowing out the pilot light on the furnace. I had to keep relighting it. We'd get heat for a little while until the wind blew it out again. We stayed all winter and roughed it out. We worked all the next summer but the house still wasn't ready to move into. Here came winter again and we decided we needed better winter quarters. I still had two empty lots down in Corpus Christie on the Laguna Madre, those lots that I bought way back in 1963. I had this brilliant idea to build another house in Corpus Christie during the winter. So, that's how we came to be building two houses at once in two different states. I always liked projects that seemed impossible. It's kind of like gambling with myself.

From audio recordings made on June 16, 2009 and September 15, 2011.

221

Two Crazy People

We pulled the camper down to Corpus and started making plans to build a house on our lots right on the water. We had to contend with a lot of bureaucratic nonsense. One time we had to get a permit for something or other and we went into this office. There was a lady sitting there issuing numbers. We walked in and she said, "Take a number."

We looked around and nobody was there.

"We're the only ones here," we said.

"Take a number."

We had to sit there for awhile until she decided to call our number. We were lucky and eventually got all our permits to build. We wrestled through it with the bureaucrats. In that area where our property was they declared that all the grass was endangered. You couldn't move a sprig of it. Luckily, where we built there wasn't any grass. They had shut other people down from building if it involved cutting down a single blade of this grass. Those bureaucrats were like spies down there. Going down the road with binoculars watching what people were doing.

This fellow bought four acres of property right close to ours. The whole lot was just a big mud hole. It was a mess. He brought in a lot of dirt to level out the property and get ready to build. It was looking a lot better. A government fellow came along and shut him down. He said it was bird habitat. I said, "There hasn't been a bird on this place in ten years. The birds don't like it here." That didn't matter. They made him pull all the dirt out and put it back to its natural, crummy-looking state.

We had to put in the very first water treatment unit. It cost us $5,000. Everyone else who had built houses before us had put in septic systems. But, they had a new regulation that said the water had to be treated before we could put it on the lawn.

"What lawn?" I said. "We don't have a lawn. It's all sand around the house. We're on the beach, for crying out loud."

"You have to put in a water treatment unit, or else you can't build." That kind of stuff went on the whole way through this building project.

They told us the house had to be twelve feet off the ground. None of the other houses around there were nearly as high as ours had to be. So, I rented a tractor and a great big auger to dig holes for the pillars. I had to sink these big pillars five feet down into the ground, every eight feet. After I got the holes dug, I took big eighteen inch timbers and dropped them down into the holes and braced them so they couldn't move. Then we mixed up cement and dumped the cement into the holes from a wheelbarrow. Then we built a platform across the pillars. It took us the whole first winter to get the pilings down and the platform built.

Then when spring came, we left everything there and went back to Trinidad to build on that house. We did everything on both houses. Eunice and I hammered every nail. I did all the plumbing and the heating. We mixed cement and poured it. We laid the tile and built cabinets. We installed the windows. I had to have someone else do the electrical, but that was about it.

Down in Corpus, it was tricky because the house was so high up in the air. Putting those rafters up, I was hanging off of those suckers twenty-eight feet up in the air. I finally was putting the last rafter on the house. I was way up there and I lifted that heavy rafter; it was a dumb move. I got a darn hernia and had to go to the hospital. I had to get that operated on; that set us back a couple of weeks.

The wind would come up every morning and it blew all day. I could hardly handle a big sheet of siding with that wind blowing. I rigged up a boat winch to pull the siding up from the ground. We pulled each sheet of siding up with that winch and then I'd run up the ladder and hammer that thing in place before the wind would catch it. We were just about finished with the Corpus house and we were waiting for a calm day to put the last piece of siding on. We waited and waited and then early one morning Eunice woke me up.

"Listen," she said. "There's no wind."

So we jumped out of bed and ran over to the house. We lifted that last piece of siding into place. That was a relief to get that done.

It took us two winters to finish the Corpus house and three summers to finish the Trinidad house. We hung onto the Corpus house for a year or so. It was real nice with a big deck. I could sit out there on that deck and look out over the water and smell the sea breeze. But, we decided to make Trinidad our permanent quarters. It was too hard to tend to the Corpus house from so far away. We sold it. We had fun building that place. People would pull up on the street and watch us from their cars. Watching these two crazy people building this house by themselves. That was a fun project.

From audio recordings made on June 15, 2009, November 30, 2010, and September 15, 2011.

That's a Good-looking Cow

When we bought the Trinidad property I wanted a place where I could build our own house, build a barn, and have some horses. About six months after we moved in to our Trinidad house, we bought two beautiful Morgan horses. They were brothers, Dick and Dan. We just loved those horses. One day my neighbor came up to our place and he asked me, "Would you like to buy a cow that's about to have a calf?"

I wasn't planning to become a cattle rancher. I knew that getting into cattle would take a lot of work. "I don't know," I told him. "What does she look like?" We went down there and I looked at this cow and I thought to myself, why, that's a good-looking cow.

"Okay. I'll take her."

We hauled her back to my place. Eunice came outside. "What's this?"

"It's a cow. She's about to have a baby calf. I bought her." "Why?"

"Look at all this beautiful grass we've got out here. It's just going to waste."

I wasn't an expert with cows. We had some on the farm when I was a kid, but that was sixty years before. I figured I knew enough, though, that I could take care of a couple of cows.

Before long, this same neighbor came and asked me to buy another cow that was about to have a calf. That's how the whole thing started. My herd started growing. Herding cows, buying and selling them. It's a tough racket, but I loved just about every cow I had. They were like my little kids.

From audio recordings made on September 15, 2011 and September 24, 2011.

225

Eighty Miles from Nowhere

One day Eunie and I were outside tending to the cows. We had eleven cows at that time. This idea just popped into my head and I said to her, "Eunie, I'm going to build a herd."

"What?"

"I want to have a real herd of cattle. I want more cows."

"You've lost your mind."

It hadn't taken long for those few cows that we had to eat all our beautiful grass down to bare dirt. I knew we couldn't really have much of a herd on the property we had.

"Let's go up to Idaho," I said. When I was a kid, we used to go up to Buhl, Idaho where Mrs. Jordan's daughter lived. I remembered all the great pastures up there.

So, we took a two week trip to Idaho to look around. We looked all over the southern part of Idaho. A realtor sent us out to this one piece of property out in the middle of nowhere that had a big old house on it. It had been a beautiful home at one time, but it was real run down. Roots of the trees had cracked the sides of the house. We went inside with a flashlight and my pistol. I didn't know what we'd find in there. The place was in pretty bad shape.

All of a sudden Eunice screamed bloody murder and jumped back about three feet.

I said, "Eunice, don't scream like that when I've got a loaded gun in my hand."

"There's an eye looking at me right through that crack in the wall."

I looked up and there was this eye peering through a hole. We went into the next room and there was a big bird sitting in a nest right by that hole in the wall. That place had been abandoned for a long time and it would have taken tons of work and money to fix it up. We went back to the realtor's office in Twin Falls and we met this guy who had just decided he wanted to sell some property he had.

"It's 300 acres with a couple of old cabins on it," he said.

226

"Let's go see it."

He didn't mention it was eighty miles from nowhere. We drove and we drove getting out there. We finally came to this place. I looked around and saw the old cabins. The grass was a foot high. He left and we pitched our tent right there inside one of the old cabins. We spent the night out there.

We got up the next morning and I thought, this is it. This is the place. It was all fenced. There was water all over the place. Some real nice springs. After coming out of the dust bowl in Trinidad, I could hardly believe it. Water and all that beautiful grass, and the mountains all around, and those two old cabins. Those cabins, that were right next to each other, had been built in 1873, but no one had lived in them since the 1930s. Those cabins were full of history. They had the original doors on them. I just loved that place.

We went back to the realtor's office and we bought the property. Then came the realization of what we'd done. We knew we'd have to work our tails off to get those cabins livable again. This was in 2002. A year before my eightieth birthday, I became an Idaho rancher.

From an audio recording made on September 24, 2011.

I Felt Like an Old Pioneer

We had a caravan going up to Idaho. Two friends drove up with us. We took the horses and all our cows. We had two horse trailers and another sixteen foot trailer and our camper. We camped out at rodeo grounds along the way so the animals could get out of the trailers.

We made it up to the property after about a week and put the animals in the corral. We woke up the next morning and the cows and horses had broken through the fence in the corral and they were all hanging around outside our camper. Maybe they were feeling lonesome in this strange, new place. We had 300 acres that was all fenced. It wasn't the best fencing. But, I didn't have to worry. The cows didn't want to go anywhere. They stuck pretty close to the cabins. I had them so tame, they'd come up every night when I'd call them and stay in the corrals. Those corrals were built in the 1870s, but they were still standing. I repaired the corral fences and the cows just took care of themselves. Before long, they started producing like mad and we had a good herd, sixty or seventy cows. I sold quite a few of them.

The main project was re-doing those cabins. We lived in the camper about a year while we renovated the cabins. I started tearing them all apart and getting rid of all the crap inside. I ripped up the floors. The rats that lived in the cabins were about ten inches long. They were big and nasty. Eunice would say, "There's one!" I'd pull out my pistol and bingo. Got that sucker. I had to stucco the whole inside of the cabins to get them rat-proof. After I stuccoed all the inside walls, an ant couldn't have gotten in those cabins. I had them foolproof. We could sleep in there and not worry about a rat chewing on our toes.

I had to work on the outside of the cabins, too. They were made of big, round logs. I had to fill up holes and put windows in the walls. I had to build a bathroom because there wasn't one inside. There was a kitchen with a couple of sinks, but no appliances. We had a deep well. It was a beautiful well with good, clear water. Very tasty. There was a pump about 150 feet down in the well. I had a generator to run the pump and bring water up to the cabins. We put a 1,000 gallon propane tank out there. We had all the modern conveniences except electricity. I used propane lamps to read at night. And, we bought a refrigerator and a deep freeze and a stove that ran on propane. That refrigerator and deep freeze were very expensive, and it was a job to keep those things running. The burners kept going out. Those were real duds. There was no heat in the cabins, so I piped heat all through the rooms. Those propane heaters that I rigged up kept the place very warm. I was kicking covers off during the night in the wintertime.

I felt like an old pioneer. It was primitive out there, but it was real nice. If you call work fun, I had fun.

From audio recordings made on September 24, 2011 and September 25, 2011.

The two cabins at the Idaho ranch

It Was a Risky Deal

This ranch where we lived in Idaho was a famous place. Brown Bench Ranch. It had tons of history. There was a big dam that Chinese workmen had built in the 1800s, all out of stone and big boulders. It was a big attraction for people. The Chinese also built a big long wall out of stones. It was such a famous ranch that we'd be sitting there minding our own business and people would come climbing over the gate. We had total strangers wander in and look over the whole place. They'd be surprised to see us and ask, "What are you doing here?"

"We live here. What are you doing here?"

"We came out to see the old cabins and the Chinese wall."

Most of the people were very nice. I'd show them all around. One time this lady in Twin Falls was telling some tourists about our ranch. "Sure," she said. "Old Irvin Hornkohl will show you around." About thirty or forty of these people from this tourist group showed up at our place. I didn't know them from Adam and I didn't know they were coming. They brought about a hundred sandwiches and two kegs of beer with them. We had a party that day. Hardly a Sunday went by that someone didn't come climbing over our gate and down the lane.

In the daytime, it was beautiful out there. The nights turned into something different. It got hairy. We hadn't been out there too long and we'd spent the day in town. We headed home to the ranch after nightfall and it was pitch black. It was about eighty miles to the ranch, twenty of it on a rough gravel road. We knew the exact mileage from the edge of the blacktop to our gate. But we still missed that darn gate. We drove back and forth for about four hours. We went all the way back to the blacktop and started over again on the gravel road. This place was so dang isolated, it was difficult to find at night. I told Eunie, "Let's just sleep in the truck and go home in the morning."

"No, we know that gate is here somewhere. Let's keep looking."

We finally found it. How, I don't know. I put out reflectors on the gate after that. I spent a lot of nights out there by myself. Even for a guy like me who was used to fighting my way through a lot of things, it could get scary. One night I was asleep in bed and all of a sudden, wham, wham, wham. Someone or something was beating on the door. I thought, at first, it could be a bear. I grabbed my pistol. I never went anywhere without a pistol. I yelled through the door.

"Who's out there?"

"This is the sheriff."

"What do you want?"

"I want to know if you've got any hunters in there."

"There's no hunters in here except me."

"Let me in."

"I'm up here in the wild by myself. I'm not letting you or anybody else in here."

Boy, he started getting angry at me. Hollering and threatening me with arrest. He finally convinced me he was the sheriff. He didn't have his patrol car, of course, because the gate was locked and he had to leave it on the road. I finally let him in and told him, "If you live out here long enough, you'll be just like me. You won't trust just anybody. Especially in the middle of the night." He said he was looking for two lost hunters. I told him he should check the casino.

I wasn't too far off thinking it was a bear knocking on my door. We saw bears up there and wolves and cougars and rattlesnakes. And the ravens. Those suckers were big. These great big ravens would dive down and attack our little newborn calves. I had a .410 shotgun but that wouldn't even put a dent in those ravens. I had to buy a 12 gauge to handle the ravens. All in all, it wasn't the most hospitable place in the world. It was rather dangerous.

We'd been up there about four years and Eunice fell inside the cabin and got a blood clot in her leg. She had to go

231

to the hospital in Twin Falls. That just started a downward spiral of what we were up against out there. The doctor said, "She can't be that far from town. Nobody can get to her if she gets another blood clot." It would take us about two hours to get to town. So, we decided to sell the place and go back to our Trinidad house permanently. I sold that ranch immediately. It was a hot item. If I'd have had two more places like that, I could have made some real money. I could have been a big cattle dude if I'd stayed right there on that property. Eunice said I could have been dead, too. That was true. It was a risky deal.

From audio recordings made on February 17, 2011, September 24, 2011, and September 25, 2011.

My Next Project

When I think back on my life, I'll admit it – I'm no brilliant scholar. Most of the things I accomplished didn't take brilliance, but they took perseverance. Anybody can start something, but it takes guts to finish it. People tell me I'm too old to be doing what I'm doing. People say things about me. "Oh, he shouldn't have that ranch. That's too much for an old man." I can't help what people say. I'm eighty-eight years old. It's just a number, that's all.

I'm very happy that we wrote this book. I'd thought about writing a book for a long time. People would say to me, "Irvin, why don't you put all these stories down in a book?" But I never figured it would happen. I didn't know what it would involve, how to do it. It's quite an undertaking. Then I met Mary on that airplane that day. On Pearl Harbor Day. Neither one of us knew it then, but that started it off. It took us three years to put this book together, but we made it through. We got it all down. I owe so much to Mary for doing this.

Now, I'm planning to go out and be a salesman for this book. That's my next project, crazy or not.

From audio recordings made on August 11, 2011, August 31, 2011, and September 25, 2011.

Irvin, August 2011

(Photo by Debbie Wiens)

Visit **www.manzanoalley.com** to learn more about Irvin and his adventures. On the website you'll find:

- A photo gallery of Irvin's life
- News about appearances and book signings
- Book ordering information
- Information about inviting Mary to speak to clubs and groups about the process of turning oral history into a written biography